SPERM COUNTS

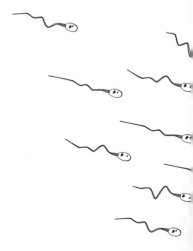

INTERSECTIONS
Transdisciplinary Perspectives on Genders and Sexualities

General Editors: Michael Kimmel and Suzanna Walters

Sperm Counts: Overcome by Man's Most Precious Fluid
Lisa Jean Moore

LISA JEAN MOORE

SPERM COUNTS

Overcome by Man's Most Precious Fluid

New York University Press • *New York and London*

NEW YORK UNIVERSITY PRESS
New York and London
www.nyupress.org

LIBRARY OF CONGRESS CATALOGING-IN-PUBLICATION DATA

Moore, Lisa Jean, 1967–
Sperm counts : overcome by man's most precious fluid / Lisa Jean Moore.
    p. cm. — (Intersections: transdisciplinary perspectives on genders and sexualities)
Includes bibliographical references and index.
ISBN-13: 978-0-8147-5718-5 (cloth : alk. paper)
ISBN-10: 0-8147-5718-9 (cloth : alk. paper)
1. Masculinity—Social aspects. 2. Spermatozoa. 3. Semen. I. Title.
HQ1090.M668   2007
306.7081--dc22   2007006115

New York University Press books are printed on acid-free paper, and their binding
materials are chosen for strength and durability.

Manufactured in the United States of America
10 9 8 7 6 5 4 3 2 1

For Robyn

Contents

Acknowledgments

For a person who thinks of herself as a sprinter and not a long-distance runner, writing this book has been an enormous challenge. I have learned that quick response time and short, intense energy bursts are not the qualities needed for this task, and many individuals have graciously taught me the invaluable skill of endurance. These people have encouraged me throughout the research, writing, and revision so I could cross the finish line.

This book benefited from the careful reading of many thoughtful individuals, including two anonymous reviewers for New York University Press.

In particular, I thank my mentors and colleagues Adele Clarke, Virginia Olesen, Judith Lorber, and Patricia Clough.

My undergraduate students Kristine DeLillo, Heidi Durkin, and Michael Ortiz went above and beyond their student work-study responsibilities to assist me in the preparation of the manuscript. My colleagues at the College of Staten Island and City University of New York (CUNY), including Sunny Brandler, Peter Hegarty, Victoria Pitts, Maria Sereti, and David Goode, provided insightful feedback on various chapters.

Librarians Polly Thistlethwaite at the Graduate Center of the City University of New York and Amy Levine from the Sexuality Information and Education Council of the United States (SIECUS) graciously assisted in searches for children's book materials. My appreciation to Vanessa Haney for her illustration of sperm cells. Additionally, the Professional Staff Congress CUNY Research Foundation and the College of Staten Island provided me with the necessary release time to complete the manuscript.

Monica Casper, my graduate school partner-in-crime and long-term friend, carefully advised me on several key arguments. Despite an over-busy life as an academic mom, she always comes through in the clutch.

My friends Shari Colburn, Paisley Currah, Mira Handman, and Karin Schott have been beacons when writing, and mostly revising, became dark and lonely.

Sharing a long and ongoing dialogue about sperm with my truest friend and collaborator Matthew Schmidt has been perhaps the oddest way to maintain a 15-year friendship. Our relationship has been the best outcome of this project.

Several years ago when I met Ilene Kalish, I was struck by her honesty, warmth, and intelligence. My gratitude and respect for her has only grown throughout the process of completing this book. She has carefully read and reread every word with sincere dedication. Special thanks in particular to Salwa Jabado for assisting with the images and to copyeditor Cynthia Garver for fine attention to detail.

My deep appreciation goes to Robyn Mierzwa. She reminded me to pace myself, appreciate the journey, and believe that I can finish. I dedicate this book to her.

Preface

Sperm Autobiography

I was around 6 or 7 when I was introduced to the concept of sperm. My first lesson consisted of my mother and me sitting on our "entertaining" couch in the living room. The couch, a forbidden place for me to sit and ordinarily covered with a slick plastic wrap, was now plush and inviting. Sitting there with my mother instead of on the ratty family room couch indicated the serious nature of our pending conversation. My mother seemed expectant, smiling at me enthusiastically as we opened up the pages to a new book, *How Babies Are Made.*[1] I soon learned that "the sperm, which come from the father's testicles, are sent into the mother through his penis" and that "a sperm from your father joined with an egg from your mother." The book had illustrations of chickens, dogs, and humans engaged in different sexual positions, all showing white-colored sperm in pursuit of the egg (figure 1.1).

My mother squeezed my hand and said, "This is how you got here, Lisa." I tried to picture a very tiny version of myself floating out of my father and into my mother, but it was hard to imagine. My mother said I could read the book whenever I wanted and put it in a special place for me near the couch. This book was a new treasure. To this day, I can still conjure up images of sperm as white die-cut units swimming through the insides of chickens, dogs, and humans.

Years later, in sixth grade, Timmy Lyons brought a "rubber" to school. He showed it to me in the coatroom and whispered that a man uses this to catch all the sperm so a girl can't have a baby. I giggled and asked what happened to the sperm after it went in the "rubber"? He guessed that they died. I remember feeling sad for them.

During my teen years, in addition to the pregnancy concerns of other heterosexually active girls, information and misinformation about AIDS/HIV was beginning to trickle into my high school. The

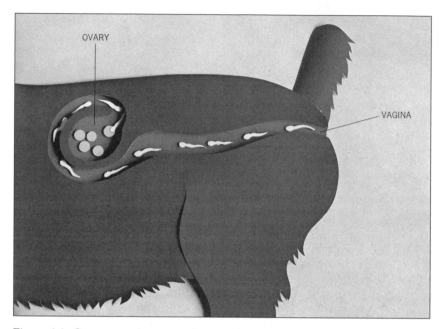

Figure 1.1. Sperm moving toward egg in dog's vaginal canal. From Andrew Andry and Steven Schepp, *How Babies Are Made*, 1968.

deadly, scary disease had something to do with sperm and transmission and anal sex: I took with me the messages that sperm was diseased and could simultaneously create a baby and kill you—two things I knew I wanted to avoid.

In college, I became interested in issues of public health and, as a graduate student, began to investigate the burgeoning sperm bank industry. At the time, sperm banks were competitive and largely unregulated enterprises that were using new technologies to create a pliable, fertile, and desirable product. Then living in San Francisco, I quickly grew familiar with a local sperm bank, the Sperm Bank of California (TSBC),[2] the only nonprofit semen bank in the United States. In operation for over 15 years, TSBC emerged out of the women's self-help movement. Their mission statement and governing values actively resist the trends of corporate America. As a budding sociologist, I decided to approach TSBC to see if I could do an on-site study of the organization, or in sociological terms, an ethnography. Unfortunately, I was denied access.

Without access to an actual sperm bank, I did the next best thing and began studying their promotional literature and soon published an article that provided a content analysis of their materials and donor catalogues.[3] As a result, I found myself asked to be on local radio programs and even landed a BBC television interview—about which my conservative and often professionally skeptical father said, "I always knew you would enter banking." One radio program arranged an on-air discussion with the executive director of TSBC. After the program, the executive director said she was impressed with my knowledge of the field and wondered if I would like to be involved with TSBC. Ironically, the director did not remember that she had denied me access to TSBC two years earlier.

It was not long before I became the organization's Board secretary. Eventually, I was elected president of the Board of TSBC and served for six years. I learned a great deal about the industry and even grew to know members of the international semen banking community.[4] Now I had the access to information I had previously only dreamed about, but I was in an ethical dilemma similar to what many medical sociologists before me had faced: How can one legitimately pursue social science research within an organization while volunteering there? Issues of confidentiality, deception, and validity reared their complicated heads and left me to use my tenure on the Board as an active community servant but a passive researcher. But my experiences at the bank as an insider to this world enabled me to learn professional rituals and gain medical expertise, and ultimately it paved the way for a subsequent in-depth research project.

After working at TSBC for so many years, it was fitting that when my partner and I decided to have children, donor insemination proved the best choice for us. As of today, my most recent contact with sperm has been through my own reproductive history. Previously, sperm was a substance I read about, felt empathy for, avoided, studied, or sold, but now I had new motives that changed my own investment in the fluid. In preparing to become the birth mother of two girls conceived through donor sperm, I was surprised by the evolutionary and competitive ideas that pervaded my thoughts while pursuing pregnancy. Like many women consciously trying to conceive, I became preoccupied with the stereotypical images of sperm swimming fast and furiously against great obstacles to penetrate my elusive egg. In my journal, I wrote:

> Each time I am inseminated, I imagine the sperm on a track and the starting gun has just sounded. I must keep my body very still and slightly elevated (I don't care what the books tell me) in order to help them get to the egg. There is such a short amount of time they will stay alive and my egg will be ready. Maybe this time just one will get there.

Our oldest daughter was conceived through a known donor during an at-home intracervical insemination. My partner used a syringe to place semen close to my cervix during peak ovulation. I still remember the first time she sucked up semen into a syringe and grimaced, "This stuff smells gross."

Despite being in San Francisco and apparently participating in what has been widely reported as the lesbian baby boom, my first obstetrics visit revealed the heterosexual paradigm. The nurse assigned to collect my vitals, asked, "What is the name of the father of the baby?"

"Oh, it was a donor."

"Okay, how do you spell that?"

I remember thinking, "What does she mean how do you spell that?" Aloud, I said, "You know a donor. A person who donates semen."

"Oh, yeah. Right. Okay." Quickly filling in my chart, she furtively glanced over and assessed me. Alone in the room, I felt judged, as if I was being evaluated for my fitness for motherhood.

Our youngest daughter was conceived two years later through an identity-release donor[5] during a physician-supervised intrauterine insemination. Every day I am grateful for the accessibility and technology that gave me access to those sperm.

Much of my professional research has had interesting personal consequences. When researching semen and pornography on campus, I have at times become concerned with the social stigma from colleagues, administrative support staff, and students. For example, since I did not have a printer in my office on campus, I had to use a shared printer in the departmental office. Printing multiple excerpts from *Adult Video News* has elicited more than a few furtive looks and awkward jokes about breaking my "bad habit" or "looks like you are having a good time in your office." And then there was the time that my university email account was shut down by the server for receiving "excessive spam," mostly pertaining to pornography.

Many of our intimate dealings with semen are shrouded in secrecy or confidentiality: reading with our mothers, sharing secrets in a coatroom, pursuing reproductive services, and assiduously avoiding and controlling sperm during adolescent and teenage sex. I share with you these stories as a way to demonstrate the ways—some obvious, some not—we come to know sperm. Of course, as women our relationship to semen is markedly different from what it is for men; boys and men are far more intimately acquainted with the substance than are girls and women. Perhaps no relationship is more shrouded in secrecy than that between a boy and his penis because masturbation, when acknowledged at all, has long been regarded as an intensely private act, sometimes as even shameful or sinful.

Since each of us originates in part from sperm, in this much, human beings have a common sperm experience. But our understandings of sperm can be quite different, as sperm is layered with meanings related to sexuality and reproduction, life and death, health and illness, masculinity and femininity. Yet, it is remarkable that a seemingly private relationship can also be a public, even communal, one. If I might offer a play on words, our understanding is "polyspermous."

Before going any further, let me set down a few definitions. First, in the contemporary Western world, there are distinct differences between sperm, semen, and ejaculation. Biologically, semen is understood as a mixture of prostaglandin, fructose, and fatty acids. Sperm, or more accurately sperm cells, make up only 2–5 percent of a given sample of semen. Semen, along with its sperm, is released through the penis, commonly through ejaculation. Contrary to popular belief, orgasms and ejaculation are separate functions, and it is possible to have one without the other. For example, tantric sexual manuals guide men in techniques to experience orgasms without ejaculating. Ejaculatory anhedonia, or anorgasmic ejaculation, describes a benign condition in which men are able to ejaculate physically but do not report accompanying feelings of release, pleasure, or orgasm.[6]

In its natural state, an individual sperm cell exists alongside millions of others in semen. Yet, sperm as individual cells are commonly separated out from semen and anthropomorphized, that is, given human qualities, in a variety of contexts. Rather than semen, most semen banks actually market and sell sperm, often associating it with a donor's characteristics and personality. Women pursuing pregnancy and fertility treatments may well visualize sperm cells dashing through tunnels and racing through obstacle courses, rather than semen floating in cervical mucus.

Human sperm is situated. That is, our understanding of sperm is based on the social circumstances in which it is "found" or represented. Our understanding of sperm in the 21st century is quite different from what it was in the 17th. In this book I examine sperm today, from a Western, primarily North American, cultural perspective to interpret the breadth of meaning associated with sperm and, by extension, with masculinity. My analysis explores how semen maintains a "fluidity of meaning," both literally and metaphorically, in the arenas of science, popular culture, criminal justice, and the reproductive marketplace. In fact, recent developments in each of these arenas have resulted in unprecedented popular access to and understanding of sperm in our everyday lives. As people attempt to establish dominant meanings of both sperm and masculinity, the dichotomies abound: sperm is hero or villain, erotic or toxic, the embodiment of male power or its downfall.

Ultimately, as I discuss in the pages that follow, semen is understood as a substance that is intimately linked to masculinity. From descriptions in children's books ("sperm can swim so fast and so far"), to allopathic and homeopathic medical textbooks ("one sperm *penetrates* the cell membrane"),[7] semen is both man's most precious fluid and his ultimate calling card. Semen left at the scene of a sex crime has become tantamount to the gold standard of incriminating evidence to be processed and distilled by bioforensic technicians. Indeed, in semen banking promotional materials, semen, specifically sperm cells, are often construed as actual men or masculine actors performing socially relevant activities. I argue in this book that by looking more closely at sperm we can learn a great deal about men and masculinity, as well as about a wide range of significant issues—from reproduction to romance and from disease transmission to forensic science. I hope this book will provide some seminal thinking on this important topic.

I

In the Beginning, There Was Sperm

It has been called sperm, semen, ejaculate, seed, man fluid, baby gravy, jizz, cum, pearl necklace, gentlemen's relish, wad, pimp juice, number 3, load, spew, donut glaze, spunk, gizzum, cream, hot man mustard, squirt, goo, spunk, splooge, love juice, man cream, and la leche.[1] I refer to the tacky, opaque liquid that comes out of the penis. Such a variety of words suggests at the very least the variety of uses and effects of sperm. As sociologists, of which I consider myself one, would be quick to point out, the very act of defining "sperm" and "semen" depends on your point of view, or your standpoint. That is, how sperm comes to be known is based on who defines it (a scientist or a prostitute), under what social circumstances it is found (at a crime scene or in a doctor's office), and for what purposes it will be used (in vitro fertilization or DNA analysis). As with its variety of names, sperm's meaning, like the substance itself, is fluid.

Yet however numerous the meanings, all sperm originates in the male body. As such, our prevailing ideas about men and masculinity are used to measure and evaluate the relative social value of sperm. This is particularly relevant at this historical moment, when the rise of sperm banks has given greater access to sperm than ever before. I would argue that this increased access, alongside a much more public presence of sperm in everyday life—think of "the stain" on Monica Lewinsky's dress or the numerous references to checking for DNA through sperm samples as reported in the news media—is being experienced by some as a threat to the power that men have traditionally wielded just by the very nature of being men. While there have been crises of masculinity throughout history, the fact that sperm can now be manipulated outside of men's bodies, can even be bought and sold like other commodities, can be tested and used as evidence in crime cases, and can be used for conceiving a baby with essentially no strings attached to the actual originator of that sperm (that is, the man), the crisis is exacerbated as never before.

POLYSPERMOUS: SEMEN IS EVERYWHERE

The bombardment of images, news stories, and scientific rhetoric about semen can sometimes seem overwhelming. Semen can be represented as engendered, malleable, agentic, emotive, instructive, sacred, profane, entertaining, controversial, empowering, dirty, clean, normal, abnormal, potent, impotent, powerful, incriminating, anthropomorphic, uniform, polymorphic, and deterministic. Even though semen is diversely, even contradictorily, represented in the preceding list of terms, the meanings of semen are deployed, on the whole, to reinforce a sense of virile masculinity. These macho representations of semen enforce ideas about the differences between men and women, in terms of both their gender and their sexuality.

This hypervisibility of stories about semen reminds us that, of course, these cells are integral to human life, but they are something more, too. They are "little soldiers," the "liquor of love," and "mighty troopers." A *New York Times Magazine* cover story in March 2006 entitled, "Wanted: A Few Good Sperm," detailed the trials and tribulations of a number of single Manhattan women who had decided to conceive through sperm donors. These "single mothers by choice" are "tired of waiting for the right guy to come along" and instead are "just looking for the right sperm."[2]

A quick survey of various media from the summer of 2005 illustrates other seminal overload. Summer books were full of sperm. Brooke Shields's postpartum depression memoir, *Down Came the Rain,* fueled by a feud with Tom Cruise, climbed the bestseller lists. In the book, Shields, struggling with infertility, laments the fate of her husband's body fluid in her vagina: the "little spermies couldn't swim upstream" because "the poor guys have been jumping into a pool with no water."[3] (Ironically, Shields and Cruise's partner, Katie Holmes, would both give birth on the same day in the same hospital a year later in the summer of 2006, proving that the "spermies" did eventually swim to their target.)

Slate deputy editor David Plotz's book *The Genius Factory: The Curious History of the Nobel Prize Sperm Bank* received rave reviews from many prestigious newspapers.[4] In this account of the Repository for Germinal Choice, which existed from 1980 to 1999, Plotz traces the creation of a sperm bank that used only Nobel Laureates as donors. Their mission was to save the gene pool by preventing genetic degradation and curbing the production of "retrograde humans." Interestingly, though, the female recipients of the prized sperm did not necessarily need to be Nobel Laureates or deemed equivalently elite. In any case, after nearly two decades, competition from other sperm banks and its own decreasing popularity compelled the Repository for Germinal Choice to close up shop. Even genius sperm sometimes can't swim.

Sperm stories also regularly pop up in newspaper headlines. Stealing a glance at the *New York Post* on the subway on July 25, 2005, I was drawn to a headline: "Pop Shock: EXCLUSIVE—Dad must pay for 'secret sperm tot.'" I inched closer to the paper through the throngs of people and read, "A Brooklyn man says his estranged wife forged his signature on a form to get his frozen sperm—and then used it to conceive his daughter. He was ordered to pay child support—and now he's filed a $9 million suit naming his wife and the fertility clinic as plaintiffs."[5] Later that week, I read an article by Katha Pollitt in *The Nation* in which she underscored the ironies of pharmaceutical funding, research, and distribution of contraceptive and sexual drugs; she exclaims, "Viagra is pro life, the Pill is pro death—sperm rules!"[6] An August 1 report on CNN recounts the all-too-familiar story of a man, Thomas Doswell, released from prison after 19 years for a rape he didn't commit: "When the tests came back last month showing that semen taken from the victim was not from Doswell, prosecutors filed motions to vacate his sentence and release him."[7] The relieved Doswell is shown embracing his family. No mention is made as to who the sperm actually came from.

Newspapers regularly report in their science sections on research studies of animal sperm competition that might explain the actions of human sperm. According to a July 2005 BBC world service report, to test the effects of microgravity on sperm, China plans to send 40 grams of pig sperm to outer space. Upon return to Earth, the astro-sperm would be used to inseminate female pigs. A *New York Times* article, "Sex, Springs, Prostates and Combat: New Studies, Better Lives," cites an experiment on heterosexual men between 18 and 35 who are asked to ejaculate after being exposed to images of competitive sexual situations.[8] The volume of their ejaculate is then measured to see if competition triggers greater seminal production. The implication is that if men produce more ejaculate (and therefore more sperm) when they feel competitive in sexual situations, this feeling will increase the likelihood of successful insemination. The dubious extension of this hypothesis is that sexual competition is rewarded in the process of natural selection.

Not to miss a sensational opportunity, the WB, the now-defunct teen television network, aired a new sitcom midseason 2005/2006 entitled *Misconceptions.* The promotional blurb states:

> Jane Leeves (Frasier) is Amanda Watson—smart, sophisticated, and a little out of touch with her 13-year-old daughter, Hopper. Amanda was ready to buy Hopper an iPod for her birthday and was shocked to find out that all she really wanted was to meet her biological father. Why wouldn't she? He sounds amazing. Hopper and Horace, Amanda's best friend (French Stewart, 3rd Rock from the Sun), have heard for years how this mystery guy is Ivy League-educated, well bred, handsome, incredibly athletic, and a successful doctor. The only problem is, Amanda doesn't actually know him. She only knows him as #431 from The Ivy League Sperm Bank and the profile that she had been given.[9]

Always looking for new story lines, clearly the television network sees the inherent dramatic possibilities of sperm banks. Although it was promptly cancelled, NBC also produced, *Inconceivable,* a show that followed the travails of a fertility clinic where an animated sperm cell popped up to introduce the on-screen chapter titles.

In television shows, news stories, and scientific studies, certain sperm stories are repeatedly played out. These stories are emblematic of how we come to know and understand sperm and men. The commonality in each story is that sperm are essential to human life. Similar to the story of Viagra, sperm have journeyed from the realm of the secretive to the realm of the communal. Just as it used to be taboo to speak about impotence, we now seemingly can't stop talking about the stiffness of penises ("Erections may last four hours," as one commercial warning notes) or the ejaculate that forcibly explodes from them.

Yet while sperm may reign supreme, arguably we live in a moment where traditionally defined masculinity can be seen as weakening. With the rise of the "metrosexual," the professional sports steroids scandals, the outing of impotence with the success of Viagra, the mainstreaming of shows like *Queer Eye for the Straight Guy,* and the arrival of even the gay cowboy with the film *Brokeback Mountain,* American popular culture continues to challenge a monolithic but oft-celebrated "rugged" heterosexual masculinity. As our ideas about men and masculinity change, our ideas about sperm—specifically, its power and value—also shift. I contend that at this moment sperm have increased visibility as never before.

Although sperm has been defined differently over time, particularly as science and technology advance, sperm as a substance has also become more malleable and flexible (or fluid) than ever before. For example, we can do more things with it—count it, capture it, dispense it—than we could 20 years ago. Sperm are still represented as strong, fast, crafty, resilient, competitive, and long lasting, as men often are, yet the confidence in those ideas seems to be eroding with technological advancements and with changes in societal mores. Sperm now have the power to convict or free men, identify paternity, and fertilize in perpetuity—enabling men beyond the grave to father children. It would seem that sperm has a life of its own. Yet all of these technological advancements have, ironically, given more power to women than to men, as women can now control and be protected from sperm in ways that were previously not available. As *New York Times* writer Jennifer Egan put it in a recent article, "Buying sperm over the Internet . . . is not much different from buying shoes."[10] With men losing control over the very substance that many would say defines them as men comes a rather unsettling state for men and manhood, with many questions left unanswered.

DIVING IN: FOLLOW THAT SPERM

Interested in these ironies, in this book I explore the power and complexity of semen. Using a "follow that sperm" approach, I first trace the historical journey of sperm from its fabulous Western bioscientific discovery to its war-weary travails in the vaginal crypt. Attaching my analytic lens to sperm itself provides interesting perspectives on how sperm "is spent" and is reabsorbed, as well as how it swims, spurts, careens, and crashes through ducts, penises, vaginas, test tubes, labs, families, cultures, and politics. Examining the science of semen historically and culturally, I show how scientific representations of sperm and semen change over time. Much like the fluid of semen itself can leak onto different fabrics and into different bodies, the meanings of semen are able to seep into our consciousness. How does sperm relate to manhood? What does it mean to be a "real" man? A "real" father?

In a sense, this book's analysis reveals how "sticky" or messy and complex masculinity is in the 21st century. I see sperm as a metaphor for contemporary masculinity: it is both valorized and reviled, representative of life and death. Yet despite its "fluid" quality, sperm is always already essentialized and relied on to tell the story of masculinity in many social arenas, including family, law, science, and the sex industry. Through these stories, as with any concept, sperm becomes institutionalized and taken for granted and, thus, self-sustaining.

My work expands on previous scholarship by analyzing how sperm is a "liminal substance" that traffics between biological and social worlds. That is, sperm is both a material and a symbolic entity, is a part of both nature and culture, and has scientific and social value. For example, anthropologist Emily Martin, in her groundbreaking article, "The Egg and the Sperm: How Science Constructed a Romance Based on Stereotypical Male-Female Roles," showed that there is no "objective and true" knowledge about fertilization by revealing the ways in which scientific knowledge is always socially and historically situated. Martin shows that the tropes of biological textbooks reveal the cultural beliefs and practices enacted in these suggestive images: sperm are strong, eggs are passive. In this book, I build on Martin's concerns about the power of metaphor in science to keep "alive some of the hoariest old stereotypes about weak damsels in distress and their strong male rescuers."[11]

Drawing on 15 years of research, *Sperm Counts* interprets the many meanings of semen in the 21st century. I examine historical documents from biomedical and reproductive scientists, children's "facts-of-life" books, pornography, the internet, forensic transcripts, and sex worker narratives. I also base the observations in this book on the time I spent doing research in sperm banks and interviewing executive directors, board members, lab technicians, and recipients—the elusive ethnographic work mentioned earlier.[12] Understanding how we biomedically, socially, and culturally produce, represent, deploy, and institutionalize semen provides valuable perspectives on the changing social position of men, male differences, and the changing meaning of masculinity.

Ultimately, sperm is not involved only in the physical reproduction of males and females but in how we come to understand ourselves as men and women. The ways in which we choose to manage and assign meaning to sperm indicates the recalcitrance of our stereotypes about gender. This gendered social order is both reinforced and destabilized by the meanings assigned to semen and the manipulation of sperm's potential.

THE MASCULINE HEGEMONY

Sociologist R. W. Connell has coined the phrase "hegemonic masculinity" to explain the inherent variations of masculinity.[13] He argues that hegemonic masculinity involves not only the domination and exploitation of men over women but also the domination and exploitation of certain kinds of men over other men. This is accomplished, in part, by instituting an "ideal type" of masculinity—that is, strong, aggressive, physically dominating, wealthy: tough men like Arnold Schwarzenegger, Ted Turner, and Michael Jordan. Today our understanding of masculinity is based on physical power, brute force, rationality, and controlled emotion. This is a hollow image, based on cultural icons that do not reflect the reality of most men's lives. Nonetheless, this ascendancy of a "man's man" is supported by social structures in which the concept of masculinity is embedded: religion, politics, and popular culture. For example, heterosexual, white, upper-middle-class, reproductive, serially monogamous men are situated "above" women and other types of men—homosexual, men of color, working-class, nonprocreative or sterile, nonmonogamous, and "perverted" men. Think George Clooney over George Costanza.

The power of the sciences to *naturalize* social relations is considerable because of their privileged position to offer "official" knowledge about our understanding of gender and sexuality.[14] Guided by feminist theory and masculinity studies, I examine how gender emerges from various representations of the "natural" fluids of men that, in turn, produce a "natural gender order." Gender is represented in scientific literature by relying on tropes and metaphors from fables, traditional stories, and familiar imagery.[15] I view sperm and semen representations as symbols of different types of masculinities. As a symbol of conception, sperm can be seen as a fierce competitor winning the conception race, a benevolent father laying down his life for creation, or an absent-minded professor bumbling his way as he is shuttled through passageways. As a symbol of infertility, sperm can be seen as an impotent wimp unable to sustain himself in the acidity of the vagina, while semen banks represent sperm as a good catch embodying all the desirable traits of humanity. A forensic representation casts sperm as a masculine threat overcome with animalistic passion that triumphs over rationality and decency. The representation of sperm in a paternity lawsuit might suggest a liar who strays from his faithful wife into the arms of another. A pornographic representation portrays sperm as a hunk of burning love for the insatiable appetite of oversexed women.

While these notions of masculinity as represented by sperm exist in real-lived human experiences, these representations are also ideal types of masculinity begging for a performance. Thus the meaning of masculinity is not concrete, consistent, and fixed; rather, since our own actions, or performances, of masculinity and femininity are ongoing, these representations are fluid and change depending on the circumstances. Although they are sometimes unintentional, the images or representations are meant to instruct or incite actual men and women. That is, there is traffic between the ideal type of masculinity and the performance of being masculine that is often assumed.

The ranking of men through masculinity creates an inherent and ongoing competition for the singular top position. Male-dominated institutions, like the medical industrial complex, biological or scientific enterprises, and the criminal justice system, often pit men against one another in their pursuit of this dominance. Men there are engaged in practices of representing other men as flawed, unworthy, or immoral. In forensic science, for example, men (and women) investigate seminal stains to prove the flawed character of other men. The sperm cells themselves can often be imbued with masculine attributions and foibles.

LEGITIMATE MASCULINITY

While researching sperm, I have been intrigued by the changing role of men in our society. I find myself reading with both fascination and irritation pop culture's accounts of how men have suffered from the feminist movement, especially the women's self-help movement. Students in my women's studies classes, especially frustrated young men, often exclaim how confusing everyday life has become, due in part to feminism. They express concerns ranging from issues of employment to childrearing and, most important, dating. My students can often find examples of cultural expressions of male angst. Movies like *Fight Club* and popular books such as Susan Faludi's *Stiffed: The Betrayal of the American Man* and Christina Hoff Sommers's *The War Against Boys: How Misguided Feminism Is Harming Our Young Men* are, to my mind, superficial, yet meaningful, illustrations of today's masculinity.[16] It seems to me there are several connections to be made between the increased knowledge about and control over sperm and the cultural anxiety men experience in contemporary societies. To offset these "masculinity-lite" or "sperm-lite" texts, I offer here a more nuanced and complicated account of masculinity in the postfeminist era.

I explore how sperm becomes a kind of elixir that helps generate not only "life" through reproduction (and technology) but also whole sets of social practices in the realm of science and gender relations. In interpreting how sperm cells are used, my work interrogates the consequences (intended and unintended) of manipulating sperm and the perpetual crises of masculinity in the 21st century. What constitutes legitimate masculinity is constantly being verified, challenged, and regulated. As knowledge about and technological manipulation of men's bodies, particularly their fluids, changes, the terms of what is considered legitimate masculinity must adapt. Examining scientific renderings of sperm, my work intends to expose the essence of male power. Remarkably, this power proves both inherently unstable and self-sustaining. In other words, it is amazing how gender hierarchies are ubiquitous and enduring, while simultaneously they are constantly in crisis. Changes in social structures and social relationships open up what it means to be a man and what constitutes the realm of legitimate masculinity. Via a spotlight on sperm stories, this book explores how the "essence" of the masculine is produced through various hierarchies and organizational structures.

We live in a male-dominated world where most men have more power than most women, and where having a penis and producing sperm is valued. However, the increasing visibility and malleability of sperm undermines that power (i.e., women can now buy sperm, and sperm can now convict and imprison men). This power has been undermined so significantly that sperm can actually serve to emasculate men. Now that women can purchase sperm and now that they are protected from it as never before, technology offers women some measure of previously denied power.

OVERVIEW OF THE BOOK

By beginning with scientific representations of semen, we witness the "discovery" of sperm and explore this discovery in an arena that has historically been considered a bastion of masculinity. Many of the earliest sperm scientists, themselves mostly men, envisioned semen as the key to reproduction: sperm was a cell that embodied a preformed individual. These scientists marveled at the sperm cells' powerful agency and self-contained role in reproduction. However, through the "progress" of technological and scientific innovation and the skillful manipulation of semen, sperm cells have now become merely raw materials that can be technologically procured, amplified, and even "programmed" for predictability. Despite the triumph of scientific ingenuity to capture and program individual sperm cells, through their studies of human sperm competition scientists represent sperm as having distinct personalities and jobs. This chapter traces the rise, fall, and resurgence of sperm as told by reproductive scientists.

After establishing the Western scientific origins of sperm and semen in chapter 2, this volume is divided into two parts. The first examines representations of sperm. In chapter 3, I examine the developmental stage where early childhood socialization indoctrinates children into the norms, values, and taboos of their culture. I investigate one source of how some children come to understand the "friendly" sperm cell. Here I trace how sperm is "taught" to young children by representing them as heroically masculine characters. In children's books, most of the images of sperm mirror the images of the men that produced them. For example, if the "dad" in the book is smoking a cigar, the sperm cell is also. Illustrations use facial characteristics or clothing to make the sperm look more human and especially more father-like. These men are always depicted as committed and fertile husbands and fathers. Children are encouraged to see sperm as an extension of men: as capable, competitive, cooperative, fast, and active. Overwhelmingly, children's books about human reproduction present insemination as a result of heterosexual, committed, intentional sex acts that are ultimately necessary for reproduction. Turkey basters and genetic profiling are simply not part of the picture. Through sampling children's books, we see the heroic sperm in action. The norms that are consistently produced are those of heterosexual desire and male dominance. Through these children's books, sperm as a character is responsible for "making you" under limited and supposedly normal conditions.

In chapter 4, I explore representations of sperm and semen that further support those norms, values, and taboos from childhood. I examine the sex entertainment industry. In the context of the post-AIDS era, the handling, both symbolic and practical, of potentially contaminated semen enables men and women the chance to wallow in taboo and forbidden juices. Specifically, I focus on the all-important "money shot," the climatic moment in a pornographic film where the man ejaculates. This glamorization of ejaculation is given a great deal of time and attention by filmmakers through acting, looping, lighting, camera angles, sound tracks, and editing techniques. Ultimately, the money shot pays homage to the virility and potency of men. In this arena, sperm in the form of the ejaculate is eroticized, practically worshipped, as the culmination of male release.

The second part of the book examines how semen, and sperm cells in particular, become objects of fascination to be examined, distilled, and dissected as evidence of greater social meaning. I argue that the fields of fertility and forensics distill sperm into an essential code or clues that can lead to significant truths about human life. This process of attributing greater social meaning to sperm is highly interrelated with prevailing notions about certain types of men.

In chapter 5, I analyze the growth of the semen banking industry, their advertising practices, and the backlash to this industry by certain fatherhood rights movements. Here sperm is represented and perceived as a commodity. Semen, the raw material in reproduction, is processed and distilled to become technosemen, a product invested with fantastic musings of hopeful parents or dreadful fears of regressive or conservative policy makers. A close look at their practices reveals that semen banks advertise sperm to prospective recipients (single women, lesbians, infertile couples) in a selective fashion. Not all men are invited to participate in this form of reproduction: "Only 4% of men who inquire [as donors] are selected" and "We usually eliminate 90% of all candidates," the ads tell us. Selected for marketing in donor catalogues and on websites based on phenotype and genotype, male bodies (with their sperm as proxy) are now represented as technological commodities that can be exchanged on the reproductive stock market. Ultimately, the market for sperm created by semen banks puts a new price tag on masculinity.

Human semen has been depicted as a "calling card" in dramatized reenactments of sexual assault cases, which are the focus of chapter 6. Furthermore, some medical examiners have suggested that the use of polymerase chain reaction (PCR)-DNA testing in forensic sciences is the only conclusive evidence in sex crimes. After an overview of the historical record of forensic discovery and the use of semen as evidence in crime investigation, my analysis focuses on the hugely popular television franchise of sex crime entertainment and the cottage industry of mail-order DNA testing. In contrast to semen banks, which use sperm to represent an ideal man or "Mr. Right," television crime shows and the marketing of do-it-yourself DNA tests use sperm as proxy for the perpetrator, the cheater, the "bad man."

Irony abounds in these representations of semen, the imagery not entirely meshing with real life. But in these times of terror, AIDS, and sexually transmitted diseases (STDs), sperm cells continue to be presented in naïve and nostalgic fashion whereby the sperm is wholly benign, productive, and happy and also as an endangered species and a malevolent threat to health and humanity. Furthermore, as men report feeling threatened in the job market, heterosexual relationships, and so on, many scientific accounts continue to render sperm as triumphant warriors. How and to what purpose do scientific sperm tales get told as victory marches? Will sperm continue to swim upstream, to find their targets, to beat out the other "fellas," and to cross the finish line and win the race? On the material level, of course they will: the human race is not likely to stop reproducing any time soon. But my concern is not whether the sperm will "win the race" but how we will continue to define "winning" and the very race itself. In that sense, this book helps explain how sperm counts, in ways as never before.

2

Lashing Their Tails

Science Discovers Sperm

Genesis 9 reads, "And God blessed Noah and his sons, and said unto them, 'Be fruitful, and multiply, and replenish the earth.'" It may seem strange to begin this chapter on the science of semen with a quote from the Bible, but it is important to remember that many of the earliest contributors to the discourse, discovery, and experimentation with human and animal semen considered themselves both scientists and clergy. Dating back to the mid-1200s, before individual sperm cells were even visible, some of the earliest recorded theories about semen were posited by religious scholars. In turn, "science" has long been cited as an authority on human bodies, including sperm, often erasing the ways in which scientists are situated in the culture. Further, it's important to note that ideas expressed in the Bible, like all philosophical, ethical, and religious beliefs, are produced in relation to the larger culture.

The work of the anthropologist Mary Douglas is instructive here. Douglas argues that "the body provides the basic scheme for all symbolism."[1] These bodily symbols located in and on the body represent profound sociocultural markers: "I suggest that many ideas about sexual dangers are better interpreted as symbols of the relation between parts of society as mirroring designs of hierarchy or symmetry which apply in larger social systems."[2] Collective representations of the body's meanings—whether religious, legal, or scientific—are created and transmitted both through institutions such as the media, the criminal justice system, and the medical industrial complex and through our own personal experiences. In terms of sperm and semen, as I show in this chapter, the past and present representations have much to do with how men and masculinity are understood, and, further, that some scientific theories, intentionally or not, perpetuate some of the most stereotypical notions of macho men and their rightful place in society.

SACRED SPERM

The medieval Italian Catholic philosopher and saint, Thomas Aquinas, wrote prolifically about the importance of seminal fluid and the morality of its ejaculation. According to Aquinas, who was greatly influenced by Aristotle, semen's intention is to produce a replica of itself, a male. Apparently, though, if the semen is "weak" or if environmental factors are not precipitous, a female might get created instead. Semen was empowered by two sources. First, semen contained and was propelled by man's life force: his spirit and his soul. Second, semen was interconnected with the forces of the universe. Aquinas wrote:

> This active force which is in the semen, and which is derived from the soul of the generator, is, as it were, a certain movement of this soul itself: nor is it the soul or a part of the soul, save virtually; thus the form of a bed is not in the saw or the axe, but a certain movement towards that form. Consequently there is no need for this active force to have an actual organ; but it is based on the (vital) spirit in the semen which is frothy, as is attested by its whiteness. In which spirit, moreover, there is a certain heat derived from the power of the heavenly bodies, by virtue of which the inferior bodies also act towards the production of the species as stated above. And since in this (vital) spirit the power of the soul is concurrent with the power of a heavenly body, it has been said that "man and the sun generate man."[3]

In his *Summa Contra Gentiles*, an exploration into the nature of God, Aquinas writes an entire chapter on "the disordered emission of semen." He argues that both masturbation and contraception are crimes against humanity, second only to homicide. Aquinas is not alone. Many biblical interpretations serve as guides for the morality of seminal discharge. Indeed, the term for masturbation, "onanism," originating from the story of Onan in the book of Genesis, refers to the sin of "spilling of the seed." God killed Onan because during sexual intercourse with his dead brother's wife, Onan withdrew his penis, spilling his seed upon the ground.[4]

The belief that semen is sacred continued to resonate in religious and cultural contexts into the 17th century, when some of the first scientific ideas about the form and function of sperm were developed. At this time, the theory of preformation asserted that within each primordial organism resided a miniature, but fully developed, organism of the same species. There were two competing theories of preformation, spermism versus ovism. Battles between the ovists, those who believe the preformed entity is in the egg, and spermists, those who believe the preformed entity is in the sperm cell, depict the different scientific constructions of how these cells embodied individual replicants of humans. Portuguese biologist Clara Pinto-Correia examined these theories and argues that they can be tied to the influence of scientific advances on religious doctrines and social practices at the time, whereby "both the old and New Testament seemed to agree on god's profound distaste for any hint of sperm waste. By the 17th century these brief passages from scripture had echoed in western morals in numerous invasive and influential ways, so the issue [of masturbation] was certainly not to be treated lightheartedly."[5]

Most consider the spermists the victors in the battle. This culminated in the 17th-century notion that women were "mere vessels" in the context of human reproduction. But the consequences were also significant for men when, by the 19th century, beliefs about sperm's value centered on what historian G. J. Barker-Benfield has called the "spermatic economy": because seminal fluid is a limited resource that, once spent, cannot be recovered, men should reserve ejaculation for vaginal sex with women. Further, because semen was believed to embody men's vital life forces, depleting one's supply on non-reproductive activities could be perceived as irresponsible at best and physically or morally weakening at worst.[6]

While medieval and early modern clerics found the fruitless "spilling of seed" to be a capital crime, the scientific validation of the spermatic economy accounts, in part, for the proliferation of anti-masturbation strategies in 19th-century Western civilization. A Swiss physician, Samuel Tissot, adopting a medical view, argued that the unnatural loss of semen weakened mind and body and led to masturbatory insanity. (His dissertation, published in 1764, was reprinted as recently as 1980.[7]) Furthermore, the laws of the "spermatic economy" accorded that such masturbation would take away from the impulse to perform civilizing work that was the true manly calling. More recently, this belief about semen loss reverberates in admonitions to athletes not to engage in sex before games because the depletion of one's semen is thought to lead to the depletion of one's energy and vitality.

Of course, official scientific knowledge about semen is produced at the same time that unofficial knowledge about semen is discovered and shared. In the case of sperm, folk ideas, remedies, and understandings of reproduction clearly indicate understanding of male bodily fluids. Over many centuries and across diverse cultures, women have attempted to block male fluid from entering their vaginas. There is evidence dating back to 1850 B.C. Egypt that women inserted a pessary, or a soft ball containing various presumably spermicidal substances, into the vagina prior to intercourse.[8] Pre-scientific medical knowledge was also available as early as 1550, when Bartholomeus Eustacus, an Italian homeopath, recommended that a husband guide his semen toward his wife's cervix with his finger in order to enhance the couple's chances of conception. This reference was the first recorded suggestion in Western medical literature that humans could control their reproductive capabilities by manipulating semen. It's worth noting that this suggestion was made without the aid of a microscope or even basic scientific knowledge about the human body.

THE SPERM CHRONICLES:
SCIENTIFIC PRODUCTION OF SPERM

As discussed in this chapter, many of the earliest sperm scientists, mostly men, envisioned semen as the key to reproduction; sperm was believed to be a cell that embodied a preformed individual, the homunculus. These scientists marveled at the sperm cells' powerful agency and self-contained role in reproduction. Today, through the "progress" of technological and scientific innovation and the skillful manipulation of semen, sperm cells become merely raw materials that can be technologically procured, amplified, and even "programmed" for predictability.

There are different scientific epochs of sperm and semen. These epochs are driven by technology, scientific advances in reproduction, and historical views of masculinity and men. As in most scientific inquiry, each epoch represents itself as an evolutionary step forward from previous knowledge. The scientific story of semen is thus a progressive one, leading to the "enlightened" place in which we find ourselves today. Scientists often comment on their predecessors as if they were ignorant or irrational in proposing "bizarre" theories. Interestingly, this retrospective judgment rarely becomes reflexive among contemporary scientists, who behave as if they are not as culturally situated as their predecessors were.

It is not a coincidence that the narrative I reconstruct here—sperm's rise to power, fall from grace, and resurrection—follows the retrospective popular cultural story of contemporary Western man's own rise to power and ongoing reaction to the perceived threat of feminism and women's empowerment. Four and a half centuries since their discovery, diagnosing, and imaging, cryo-preserved single sperm cells can now be medically injected into ova. An individual man's reproductive participation, previously perceived as imperative and essential, is now readily controlled, potentially limited, and possibly even redundant. This narrative of scientific development in the use of sperm is linked to the stories of men's relative social power in the arenas of reproduction, families, and fatherhood. The ever-expanding body of scientific knowledge about semen strives to quantify both the potent and healthy and the weak and dangerous qualities of sperm. These scientific texts, laden with unscientific qualitative subtext, assist in the social construction of sperm as "good guys" and "bad guys." That is, through analogy, sperm is transformed into either powerful hero or evil villain or is degraded through the use of feminized adjectives and adverbs. In this chapter, by moving back and forth between the creation of social and scientific knowledge, practices and procedures about sperm are situated within existing tensions over the state of contemporary masculinity.

SCIENTISTS SEE SPERM

In the 1670s a single scientific innovation—the invention of the microscope—revolutionized the natural sciences and provided an entirely new perspective for scientists studying semen. Antoni van Leeuwenhoek was for the first time able to define sperm cells based on physical observation. Leeuwenhoek's own description of spermatozoa (sperm animals), or animalcules as he called them, perhaps indicates his excitement about this breakthrough. He marvels at the effort spermatozoa make to move minuscule spaces:

> Immediately after ejaculation . . . I have seen so great a number that . . .
> I judged a million of them would not equal in size a large grain of
> sand. They were furnished with a thin tail, about 5 or 6 times as long
> as the body, and very transparent and with the thickness of about one
> twenty-fifth that of the body. They moved forwards owning the mo-

tion to their tails like that of a snake or an eel swimming in water; but in the somewhat thicker substance they would lash their tails at least 8 or 10 times before they could advance a hair's breadth.[9]

Note that in this first scientific description of sperm, "the discovery," is linked to classic phallic imagery of snakes and eels swimming furiously, rather than, for example, cells rhythmically undulating.

While the use of a microscope allowed scientists to gain incredible insight into the physical aspects of previously "invisible" organisms, they could still only theorize about sperm's exact role in reproduction. For example, building on the work of Leeuwenhoek, researcher Nicholas Hartsoeker in 1694 theorized that the umbilical cord was born from the tail of the spermatozoa and the fetus sprouted from the head of a sperm cell embedded in the uterus. During the late 1700s, Lazzaro Spallanzani, an Italian priest and experimental physiologist, conducted research on fertilization using filter paper to investigate the properties of semen. He believed that spermatic "animals" were parasites and thought that the seminal fluid, not the sperm, was responsible for fertilization of ovum. It was not until 1824 that French pioneers in reproductive anatomy, Jean-Louis Prévost, a theologian turned naturalist, and Jean-Baptiste Dumas, a devout Catholic and a chemist, repeated Lazzaro Spallanzani's filtration experiments. These scientists claimed that animalcules or sperm cells in seminal fluid fertilized female eggs.[10] By the beginning of the 20th century, two zoologists at the University of Chicago, Jacques Loeb and Frank Lillie, established that sperm was species-specific and mapped out the physiology of fertilization.[11]

As in the case of Leeuwenhoek's narrative, scientists' gendered understandings of sperm and semen sometimes "leaks through" their scientific observations. For example, the well-known reproductive researcher, Henry Latou Dickinson, in his *Human Sex Anatomy* published in 1949, described semen as "a fluid that is grayish white rather than milky; upon ejaculation its consistency resembles a mucilage or thin jelly which liquefies somewhat within three minutes after emission, later becoming sticky."[12] It is interesting to consider these linguistic cues about sperm. They seem to be connected to cultural and historical understandings of masculinity. For example, Dickinson assures readers that semen is not "milky"—suggesting breast fluid, perhaps. Rather, semen is a "mucilage," or strong adherent substance.

THE FERTILITY FACTOR

In the 20th century, many innovations in sperm research have emerged out of scientists' attempts to understand male infertility. Men exposed to both environmental and occupational toxins have reported consistently higher rates of infertility, yet there is no universal agreement as to its cause.[13] There has been much debate in the fields of epidemiology, toxicology, and infertility regarding this increasing rate of men's infertility. As male fertility continues to be compromised by what some presume to be increasing environmental toxins, patients and researchers will more assiduously pursue biomedical solutions.

Richard Spark's review of the male fertility literature suggests that for global sperm count "the persistent trend is unquestionably downward."[14] With such a wide variety of risk factors, it's not surprising that men's fertility has become increasingly compromised. For example, some diseases lead to male infertility; these include cystic fibrosis, sickle cell anemia, and some sexually transmitted diseases. Environmental factors such as pesticides and herbicides (including estrogen-like chemicals), hydrocarbons (found in products like asphalt, crude oil, and roofing tar), heavy metals (used in some batteries, pigments, and plastics), and aromatic solvents (used in paint, varnish, stain, glue, and metal degreasers) have all been suspected of lowering sperm counts and damaging morphology.[15] Furthermore, men and boys may lower their sperm count through tobacco exposure, whether chewing or smoking,[16] and prenatal exposure to tobacco has been shown to lower sperm counts in male offspring.[17] Excessive alcohol consumption, marijuana smoking, and obesity also affect sperm counts and sperm performance. Endurance bicycling has been shown to significantly alter sperm morphology.[18] Researchers are now calling for studies of humans to determine if storing cellular phones near the testicles in the front pocket of pants decreases semen quality.[19]

Interestingly, many of the infertility risk factors cited here involve behaviors, occupations, or activities that are commonly associated with stereotypical notions of masculinity. As reported in many sociological and psychological studies, however, women overwhelmingly bear the blame of infertility and the brunt of more invasive treatments. Even though infertility is typically explained as one-third male factor, one-third female factor, and one-third unknown, women self-report feeling as if it is their responsibility and their failure when reproduction does not occur. But clearly male bodies, too, can be implicated by infertility, and men experience stigma from being diagnosed with low sperm counts. Indeed, in a clinician's guidebook to diagnosing motility problems, Spark instructs that low-motility sperm "appear to move as if befuddled. They possess no purposeful forward motion and occasionally exhibit circular or erratic movement patterns."[20] What happens when the performance of masculinity produces what is perceived as a profoundly "unmasculine" result in the form of lower sperm counts and even infertility? Individual men have reported psychological consequences of low sperm counts in the form of humiliation, despair, and depression.[21] Indeed, declining sperm counts matter to the social body, as well as to individual bodies.

NORMALIZING SPERM—AND MEN

From their humble beginnings in the 1700s to today, scientific representations of sperm have come a long way. What was once a science based on subjective narratives, sketches, and visual observation only is now a probabilistic system that understands men's fertility based on a wide variety of quantifiable parameters. Now, the parameters of semen analysis have expanded to include volume, pH, viscosity, sperm density, sperm motility, viability, and sperm morphology.

The first diagnostic tool to be used in the detection of male infertility was the "spermatozoa count," or sperm count, developed in 1929 by scientists D. Macomber and M. Sanders.[22] Sperm count was used for decades as the primary tool in measuring male infertility. However, clinical endocrinologist Richard Spark contends that "this no longer is sufficient, for recent advances in endocrinology, genetics, immunology and embryology have established a broader base for the differential diagnosis of male infertility."[23] Imaging technologies, such as electron microscopes and other devices, create new opportunities to produce scientific knowledge about sperm. For example, biochemists can measure the components of human seminal plasma; one textbook listed 35 different elements of semen and their referent anatomical production mechanisms.[24]

Currently, the two most common assessments of sperm's relative health are motility and morphology testing. Sperm motility can be measured quantitatively by counting the number of inactive sperm or

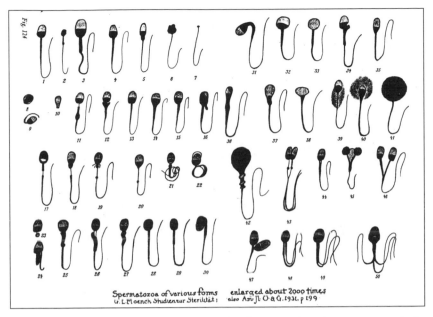

Figure 2.1. Scientist G. L. Moench's sketch of 50 variations in sperm morphology. From Henry Latou Dickinson, *Human Sex Anatomy*, 1949.

qualitatively by assessing the type of movements sperm make. Scientists' efforts to measure the distance and speed of sperm movement have been remarkably varied and numerous. For example, some recent methods used to measure sperm motility have been kinematics of flagellar undulations, computerized method, laser doppler velocimetry, and microchip assessment. There are qualitative evaluation methods as well. Some men who have lower sperm counts are capable of fertility, but it is assumed that they rank highly on either (or both) motility or morphology. It is often said in the fertility industry that the quality of sperm is more important than the quantity.

Morphology describes the shape of a cell. The first attempt to classify sperm cells' morphology was in the 1930s, when scientist G. L. Moench sketched out 50 variations in sperm morphology with names such as micro-sperm, megalo-sperm, puff-ball, and double neck (figure 2.1).[25] Today, scientists typically define normal shape as a sperm cell having an oval configuration with a smooth contour. The acrosome, a cap-like structure on the sperm's head, containing enzymes that help penetration of the egg, is well-defined, comprising 40–70 percent of the

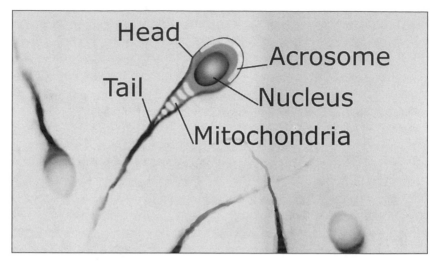

Figure 2.2. Sperm cell with parts labeled; rendered by Vanessa Haney.

head. Further, there cannot be any abnormalities of the neck, midpiece, or tail and no cytoplasmic droplets of more than half of the size of the sperm head. Given this definition of normal shape, a semen sample is considered to have a normal morphology when at least 12 percent of sperm cells are of normal shape (figure 2.2).

Intensified efforts to scientifically comprehend human semen appear to be consistent with the evolutionary logic of scientific progress. Measuring and evaluating the size, shape, and speed of sperm are a few of a number of scientific techniques that are aimed at constructing the health and the pathologies of sperm. One example of how knowing, naming, and diagnosing semen's pathological forms is produced in interaction with existing beliefs about "pathological" men is evident in an infertility textbook for medical practitioners. Spark's 1988 book on infertile men includes a chapter encompassing sophisticated techniques for medically managing infertility entitled "Coping with the Hopelessly Infertile Man." The use of the terms "coping" and "hopeless" indicate the threat to masculinity that is assumed by the lack of fertility. For example, the crossover to popular culture gives us the pejorative vernacular of "shooting blanks," which refers to men's inability to deliver, and "live ammunition," which refers to providing fertile sperm when using their penis.

In an article called "Picking a Ripe One: A New Strategy for Selecting Sperm," fertility scientists' gendered understandings of sperm are revealed through interviews. For example, Patricia Salig of Duke University Medical Center describes the process of selecting sperm: "The problem is how do you identify the good guys and then be able to use them. That's the hardest part in developing a sperm maturity test."[26]

An important part of the experience of male infertility is the projection of the sperm's characteristics (weak, slow, invalid) onto the men who produce them. I have discussed how this process challenges and even disables certain notions about hegemonic masculinity. There is another layer to this story about masculinity, though: technological advances and the creation of new tools that enable science-assisted human reproduction (such as human cloning) provide opportunities for certain men (heterosexual or married, wealthy, and able-bodied) and not others to reproduce, regardless of the quality of their sperm. With increased knowledge about and control over sperm in the context of male infertility, the standards of what counts as masculinity must adapt.

ICSI AND MALE FERTILITY

Each technological conception of semen enables new strategies to further measure, define, control, and use sperm. Similar to the evolution of systems that define and classify normal sperm, semen manipulations have proliferated from the "low-tech" donor insemination, intracervical, or intrauterine, to the "high-tech" intracytoplasmic sperm injection, where a single sperm cell is injected into an oocyte, commonly called an egg. These innovations related to human sperm are not isolated events but, rather, part of sweeping technical advances into human reproduction, with profound implications for men and masculinity.

Available since 1992, one of the most recent innovative procedures is intracytoplasmic sperm injection (ICSI).[27] This procedure is performed by a physician for selecting a sperm cell from the testes or epididymides for direct injection into the egg. Now subfertile men (defined as those men who produce some sperm with the correct morphology and may eventually achieve pregnancy with a partner without medical intervention) as well as men with an infertility diagnosis (who are still able to produce a few sperm cells but are unlikely to achieve pregnancy) are able to participate in human reproduction. Notably, it is the women's body that must be treated through implantation of embryos to correct male infertility. ICSI has complex implications for men and masculinity: the immense power of ICSI to "restore" men's fertility (and, simultaneously, their masculinity) is undermined by the fact that real social barriers make ICSI available only to certain men. In reading scientific and popular accounts of ICSI, I have noted with interest the celebratory spin that is used to emphasize the effect of ICSI for infertile men. It is not unlike marketing messages used in ads for Rogaine and Viagra: "Hallelujah, you too can feel like a man again!"[28]

Increasing levels of male infertility have driven scientists to produce a variety of biomedical solutions, including ICSI and sperm cryopreservation. On their own, these solutions offer individual men the opportunity to reclaim or repair their masculinity. However, these technologies and treatments have the potential to be used in combination for very different purposes, again producing unintended consequences for men and threatening notions of hegemonic masculinity. For example, while ICSI is considered by some sperm banks to be a potential threat to their livelihood, it could also be seen as a boon to the sperm banking industry: as experts in the cryopreservation of sperm, these banks could use ICSI as an opportunity to expand their range of services. The combination of these technologies has the potential to make men unnecessary in reproduction. This seemingly sensational statement is based on a few simple facts: cryopreserved sperm has no known expiration date, sperm banks across the globe have hundreds of thousands of vials of semen with millions of sperm cells encapsulated in each vial, and ICSI only requires one sperm cell per injection in the ovum.

While the implication is that for the purpose of reproduction, actual men could be considered redundant, of course this interpretation of ICSI has revolutionary potential for the creation of families, the roles of men and women, and the organization of social power.[29] How will actual men respond to this notion that previously procured sperm could be used to reproduce without them? Could this free-agent sperm cell now be a threat to actual men?

We need not wait until the discussion or application of this idea becomes commonplace, as many have already lamented the ways in which new reproductive technologies have obliterated the sanctity of fatherhood. For example, reactions to single women and lesbians choosing donor insemination (DI) to rear and raise children without men illustrates the supposed incredible threat that these families pose to fatherhood and masculinity (this is explored in chapter 3). In his scientific textbook, *Reproductive Tissue Banking: Scientific Principles*, Armand Karow suggests:

These technologies have caused Americans and many other people to ponder anew concepts of fatherhood, motherhood and childhood. Is it acceptable for a single woman, even a lesbian, to become pregnant with donor semen in order that she will not have to share parenthood with a man? . . . Should offending science be prohibited in the laboratory? Will these technologies explode into social catastrophe? Society evolves and matures in its understanding of its resources. At one time humans feared supernatural dragons of land, sea and air. Maturity and science conquered this fear and harnessed resources of nature.[30]

Judging from Karow's comments, "offending science," which allows even lesbians to get pregnant, was potentially destabilizing to an assumed sense of normality.

HONORABLE DEATH, KAMIKAZE SPERM

Beyond the arena of reproductive science, other scientific representations of sperm are being constructed. Particularly salient at this historical moment, given the current crisis in masculinity, is the way sperm competition theory is being used to explain and promote certain ideas about human sexuality, relationships, and reproduction. As with fertility science, the projections of behavior, motive, and character flow freely between sperm cells and the men who produce them. New renderings of sperm competition theory have taken this transference a step further.

In the late 1960s and early 1970s Geoff Parker, a scientist researching dungflies, articulated a theory about competition between ejaculates of different males for the fertilization of the egg. Sperm competition occurs when sperm from two or more males is in the female reproductive tract at the same time. His work in the field has earned him the title "the father of sperm competition" by fellow scientists.[31] Theories of sperm competition are predominantly tested and studied by evolutionary biologists and zoologists studying insects, birds, and nonhuman animals. Scientists have documented sperm competition in mollusks, insects, and birds and, using this data, have inferred that sperm competition occurs in humans as well.[32] Many scientists theorize that female sexual infidelity is the context for sperm competition.[33]

Expanding on this research, Tim Birkhead, a British behavioral ecologist, published *Promiscuity: An Evolutionary History of Sperm Com-*

petition in 2000. The book primarily explores the role of sperm competition and sperm choice in animal sexuality without a great deal of extrapolation to human sexuality. Indeed, Birkhead claims that to overgeneralize outside of particular species is intellectually dangerous and scientifically irresponsible. But evolutionary biologists Robin Baker, interestingly once an instructor of Birkhead, and Mark Bellis in their book *Human Sperm Competition: Copulation, Masturbation and Infidelity* have done just that. They apply the scientific principles of sperm competition through the generous extrapolation of animal models and behavior to humans. Baker and Bellis claim that human sperm competition is one of the key forces that shapes genetics and drives human sexuality. Their metaphor for human sperm competition is strategic warfare where sperm range from generals to enlisted soldiers, tragic heroes to victorious conquerors.[34] Written in a casual and accessible style with many illustrations and diagrams, this work depicts the crossover between hard science and pop science.[35]

Even if the science is questionable, the potential popularity of Baker and Bellis's book is understandable. Generally, in their ongoing attempts to figure out their place in the natural order, people derive great pleasure in having their beliefs about the origin of behavior proven through observations of animals. Donna Haraway, feminist biologist and political theorist, carefully examines the conventions of animal to human extrapolation. Haraway demonstrates how both scientists and laypeople have collaborated on using primates to understand human behavior, particularly the sexual nature of female primates as extrapolated to humans.[36] Because these scientific observations about animals are viewed through our cultural mediations of race and gender socialization, what might be observed as supposedly naïve animal behavior is actually misperceived. Similarly, the developmental psychobiologists Gilbert Gottlieb and Robert Lickliter have suggested that endowing animal models with explanatory power, such as providing data for extrapolation to human behavior, is incorrect. They note that "animal models of human development are at their strongest in providing general, food-for-thought propositions about human behavior and psychological functioning rather than specific or homologous exemplars. Whether these propositions turn out to be relevant to human development and behavior can only be answered by human-based studies."[37]

Although Baker and Bellis's theories and methodologies have been criticized, their work is still making a splash in the United States and

Britain.[38] Indeed, their ideas are taken seriously by popular writers and physical anthropologists. Baker and Bellis's stated aims are to offer a "purely scientific understanding of the reproductive behavior of humans and other animals" and to possibly "revolutionize the medical approach to infertility."[39] However, their interpretation of biomedical evidence is rife with sociobiological claims about how human behavior emerges from the seemingly conscious motivation of individual sperm cells. From the start, this book relies on evolutionary and genetic language, claiming that men and women are "programmed to behave" in predetermined ways "in sexual matters." For example, human mate-guarding, whereby the male species shields the female in order to reduce the probability of sperm competition, is proposed in this book by extrapolating from squirrel data. One claim from these data and a methodologically questionable survey[40] is that "some form of mate-guarding behavior is a nearly universal feature of the sexual programming of modern male humans."[41] The book can also be read as a relationship manual to aid in the understanding of the enigmatic opposite sex.

The risk of sperm competition is thought to have influenced many aspects of sexuality, including sperm and the ejaculate along with innumerable other aspects of male and female anatomy and physiology. Thus, sperm competition may be argued to promote highly competitive ejaculates and to shape anatomical devices such as the penis and vagina, thereby generating a whole array of copulatory behavior.[42]

At its inception, this book uncritically presents sperm competition, extrapolating liberally from bioscientific research primarily based on nonhuman models to grand theories of human behavior devoid of sociological insights. There are problematic statements that assume girls and women profit from sperm competition regardless of how sperm was placed in their bodies (consensually or nonconsensually) such as "a female who promotes sperm competition generally increases her chances of being fertilized by the male with the most competitive sperm. Whatever the origins of any difference in sperm competitiveness, the female can only benefit."[43] If females can only benefit from sperm competition from multiple partners, what happens in instances where multiple ejaculates are forced on women, such as gang rape?

Reminiscent of feminist anthropologist Emily Martin's work deconstructing reproductive textbook descriptions of fertilization as a romance between the sperm and the egg,[44] Baker and Bellis, without self-reflexivity, create scenarios where sperm are anthropomorphized to the degree that they have almost superhuman agency.

> As an analogy, let us compare a person (= DNA) leisurely driving a car (= sperm) uncontested from A (= vagina) to B (= site of fertilization) with the same person in a rally car racing to arrive at B ahead of numerous other hostile competitors from one or more opposing teams (= sperm competition). In both cases, only the car that arrives at B at precisely the right moment will receive a prize (= egg). However, the requirements, resources, and strategies necessary to attain a prize in the second scenario are infinitely greater than in the first, even though in the first the person may stand a better chance of completing the journey.[45]

Here, the masculine imagery of car racing is used to bring to mind speed, fierce competition, and danger. Not only are Nascar-racing tropes used in this text, but also WWII fighter jets, football, and nuclear destruction are used to illustrate sperm behavior. And what can we learn from these analogies? Completing the journey is not as important as getting there first. Faster, rally-racing sport cars are able to capture the checkered flag faster than leisure sedans can. These tropes use sperm to embody hegemonic male ideals of winning, competing, racing, destroying, and attacking.

The centerpiece of the Baker and Bellis book is the development of a theory and coining of the term the "kamikaze sperm hypothesis" (KSH), which suggests that animal ejaculates consist of different types of sperm, each programmed to carry out a specific function. Some, often very few, are "egg-getters," programmed to attempt to fertilize the female's eggs. The remainder, often the vast majority, is programmed for a kamikaze role. Instead of attempting to find and fertilize eggs themselves, their role is to reduce the chances that the egg will be fertilized by sperm from any other male.[46]

Through their KSH, Baker and Bellis create a means to explain polymorphism of sperm, and thus they rescue all morphs of sperm from the label of useless and provide job descriptions: "In the past, 'non-normal' sperm have been considered to be unwanted passengers in the ejaculate; unavoidable deformities that are a hindrance to conception. Our Kamikaze Sperm Hypothesis (KSH) argues otherwise. Each sperm morph has a part to play in the whole process of sperm competition and fertilization."[47] That is, each morph is part of a team in pursuit of the larger goal of allowing the chosen sperm to fertilize the egg. In a battlefield motif, all sperm work in a concerted effort to benefit the chosen one's ability to capture the castle. Old and young sperm are "recruited" from the ejaculate: normal and non-normal morphs have purpose. And while "younger" sperm cells may be more likely to reach an egg, it is important to understand the ways in which the scientist delivers this information to us.

The authors discuss the credentials of these morphs of sperm in detail using football or war analogies to describe the "division of labor." For example, sperm cells labeled as the seek-and-destroy sperm engage in "head-to-head combat," where the acrosome on the sperms' heads are described as if they "were in effect carrying a bomb on their heads."[48] Since sperm occupy two primary statuses, "egg-getters" and "kamikaze," Baker and Bellis provide readers with detailed typologies of each. Egg-getters are thought to be "macros"—sperm with oval-shaped heads that are longer and wider than those of other sperm. In addition to the normal challenges of sperm achieving fertilization, according to the KSH, egg-getters must overcome even more tremendous obstacles: "Throughout the whole journey, the successful egg-getter has to avoid the seek-and-destroy attention of both sperm from other males and even 'family planning' from some within its own ejaculate."[49]

The use of the term "kamikaze" appears to be an odd choice for scientists to use when developing a scientific theory of sperm. During World War II, Vice Admiral Takijiro Onishi, commander of Japan's First Air Fleet, selected volunteers from his troops to become suicide pilots to fly planes loaded with bombs into allied ships.[50] Called "kamikaze" (translated as "divine wind") fighter pilots, due to their culture's high honor of such a mission, Admiral Onishi had more volunteers than planes available—these were "real men" who used their bodies for the glory of their nation. These men did not walk away from the ultimate challenge and risked all to protect their homes. In using the term "kamikaze," Baker and Bellis suggest that this is a revered job in the division of labor of reproduction. The honor bestowed on the men who flew these self-sacrificing missions is transferred to the valiant sperm that die during their mission to fertilize eggs. Is fertilization, then, a bombing mission where sex and violence get conflated once again?

Kamikaze sperm are subdivided into two more specific groups: blockers and seek-and-destroy sperm. The first type, the blocker sperm, gets in the way of another male's sperm on their way to the "cervical crypts." Coiled-tail "old and dying sperm" are often blockers as it is a "sedentary activity."[51] Images come to mind of aging football players blocking access to the football by the competitors so the spry quarterback can toss the egg to the rightful recipient—the fastest, fittest, wide receiver, who is gracefully avoiding collision with competitors' sperm/player.

The second type, the seek-and-destroy sperm, roams around seeking another male's sperm and through the use of "highly destructive proteolytic enzymes produced by their acrosomal complex" incapacitate other sperm.[52] The authors hypothesize that seek-and-destroy sperm from one male transforms, through an unknown mechanism, from oval-headed to round-headed and releases its acrosome to kill other sperm: "We have observed sperm appear, in effect, simply to drop dead after having swum past another sperm."[53] Moreover, sperm are lethal and murderous when they are in pursuit of a valuable goal. The authors contend that "chemical warfare" and "head-to-head combat" lead to the transformed sperm being less fertile, as well as to higher rates of mortality for all sperm. The authors identify the seek-and-destroy sperm in part by their shape: tapering, pyriform, and modal oval-headed. These representations also seem at least somewhat informed by computer and video games, another masculine pursuit—such as the 1980s favorite Pac Man, featuring little creatures that gobble up other creatures onscreen.

Within the kamikaze sperm hypothesis, no sperm morph is unaccounted for in the division of labor and the quest to fertilize the egg. Even the old, sedentary, and dying sperm cells can go out with glory by blocking the access of other sperm to the egg. The competitive nature of men against men and sperm against sperm echoes certain notions of hegemonic masculinity, discussed earlier, whereby the most superior sperm will win and all men are born to fight.

According to these authors, sperm (with no mention of the egg) are singularly responsible for the evolution of human sexuality. There is no discussion of outliers, non-procreative sexuality, or sophisticated technological manipulation of sperm. These omissions are not surprising, though, when Baker and Bellis's use of sperm competition theories is understood as a response to current crises in masculinity, especially around reproductive agency. Baker and Bellis are responding with two powerful messages about men's participation in reproduction. First, by endowing all sperm with function and agency, they reject the accepted scientific notion of "good" and "bad" sperm in the context of male infertility and thereby neutralize the threat to masculinity that the projection of these characteristics onto men represents. Second, by positioning sperm, with all of its hegemonically masculine characteristics in attendance, as the

Figure 2.3. A is the artificial vagina that is filled with a semen-like substance, B and D are phalluses with coronal ridges, and C is the control phallus without the ridge. From G. G. Gallup, R. L. Burch, M. L. Zappieri, R. A. Parvez, M. L. Stockwell, and J. A. Davis, "The Human Penis as a Semen Displacement Device," in *Evolution and Human Behavior* 24 (2003): 277–289.

lone driver of human sexuality, Baker and Bellis effectively put men—rather than sperm banks, doctors, and women—back in control of human reproduction. These theories may also precipitate change because they motivate others to see their sperm as having agency of their own. It is almost as if some men wish to retain an idea that the sperm commandeers a man's body and that the sperm's "drive" compels men to behave in particular ways. Sperm with a mind of its own (similar to another male body part) must be discharged into as many women as possible.

RISK OF THE OTHER GUY'S SPERM

While there may be skepticism about the validity of human sperm competition theories, experimental research takes these theories quite seriously. Presuming that human sperm competition exists, studies have been designed to explore the role of human sperm competition in the context of male anatomy, male psychology and behavior, and human reproduction. One such study hypothesized that the human penis may have evolved as a semen displacement device.[54] A research team created artificial anatomical models of male genitalia complete with simulated semen to test the hypothesis that the human penis is designed to displace semen deposited by other men in the reproductive tract of a woman (figure 2.3).

The coronal ridge is the bulging part of the penis; it can work in two ways. As a vacuum inside the vagina, when the penis is pulled back, it sucks out everything inside the vagina, much like a plunger sucks back anything in a pipe. Or, the other man's semen gathers on the back of the coronal ridge, and then the penis acts as a "scooping" device, similar to a ladle pulling soup out of a pot: "If a female copulated with more than one male within a short period of time, this would allow subsequent

Figure 2.4. The "semen" is displaced by one of the phalluses with a coronal ridge after the experiment. From G. G. Gallup, R. L. Burch, M. L. Zappieri, R. A. Parvez, M. L. Stockwell, and J. A. Davis, "The Human Penis as a Semen Displacement Device," in *Evolution and Human Behavior* 24 (2003): 277–289.

males to 'scoop out' semen left by others before ejaculating."[55] Their results demonstrated that a model penis with a glans and coronal ridge which most closely resembled a real human penis displaced significantly more simulated semen (91 percent) than did a model without a glans and coronal ridge (35 percent), suggesting that the penis is physically designed to act like a plunger, displacing the sperm of other men (figure 2.4). The study drew on key assumptions of human sperm competition theory in attempting to demonstrate that men can and do use their penises—that, in fact, the shape of the penis itself has evolved—to try and displace other men's semen when they suspect their mate has been unfaithful.

In 2005, an international team of psychologists and biologists designed an experiment to test hypotheses regarding male psychology as correlated with sperm competition. They state, "Sperm competition also may have fashioned a psychology that generated specific corrective behaviors designed to increase the likelihood that a man's ejaculate would out-compete rival sperm."[56] The study participants were 305 men in a committed, sexual relationship with a woman (defined as being together at least one year). These men were asked to fill out a self-administered questionnaire regarding their sexual practices and their beliefs about their partner's attractiveness. The mean age of the sample was 25.8 years, and the mean age of female partners was 24.6 years. The researchers hypothesized that men at a high recurrent risk of sperm competition, measured by their assessment of the attractiveness of the female partner, would employ preventive and corrective behaviors to avoid sperm competition. These behaviors included mate-retention tactics measured by variables such as verbal possession signals, physical possession signals, and possessive ornamentation (wearing objects or clothing that signify attachment). Semen-displacing behaviors measured by length of sexual intercourse and the thrusts of the penis during intercourse were also analyzed. Researchers found some correlation between sperm competition and preventive and corrective behaviors.

Another group of evolutionary psychologists conducted research to document human male psychology adaptations to decrease the likelihood that a rival male's sperm will fertilize a female partner's egg(s).[57] One research finding was that men who spent a greater amount of time away from a female sexual partner rated their partners as more attractive and reported greater interest in copulating with them. From this finding, researchers suggest that the perception of a partner as more attractive, combined with a greater interest in sex, may motivate a man to copulate with his partner as soon as possible. This greater interest in sex could then place his sperm in competition with any rival sperm that may be present in his partner's reproductive tract. As scientific validation of "absence makes the heart grow fonder," this research contributes to the growing evolutionary literature of sperm competition.

Though not specifically about human sperm competition, in *The Other Guy's Sperm: The Cause of Cancers and Other Diseases*, Donald Tyler, a clinical instructor at the University of Utah's medical school and a practicing urologist, argues that "foreign sperm are the missing link in causes of diseases. They probably are the major cause of cancers and many other devastating diseases."[58] Foreign sperm, defined as any sperm in a woman, and another male's sperm in a man, pools inside a woman's vagina and enters into non-homosexual men by traveling up the urethra to invade the lining of the genitourinary tract and the lymphatic and circulatory systems. According to Tyler, sperm invading cells other than ova could account for all the characteristics of malignant cells, including their rapid uncontrolled division and abnormal numbers of chromosomes.

Tyler argues that sperm then invade the body (particularly the male body since female bodies seem to have some unexplained defense against sperm[59]). Similar to how the body may reject a tissue or organ transplant, the body attacks the sperm cell, which then leads to inflammation and destruction of healthy tissue. When antibodies attack the other guy's sperm, they may also attack cells and organs of the host body, causing autoimmune diseases. In effect, Tyler takes human sperm competition even further, portraying sperm as lying in wait in female receptacles, entering men's bodies and attacking, ultimately destroying the integrity of the human body.

POPULARIZING HUMAN SPERM COMPETITION

Antifeminist backlash expressed in scientific and medical discoveries and popularized through mass media occurs throughout Western history. As historian G. J. Barker-Benfield explains during the 19th century, the growth in women's rights "intensifies male anxieties" and greatly influences prevailing notions of men's, and more extensively women's, reproductive capacities.[60] Sociologist Michael Kimmel's research reveals that "a strongly misogynist current runs through a number of religious tracts, medical treatises, and political pamphlets of the late nineteenth century. Opponents of economic, political, and social equality between men and women almost always resorted to arguments about the supposed natural order of things as counters to these social trends."[61] So while this practice of male anxiety over women's growth in social power is not new, in the case of sperm competition it takes on a new twist. In these cases, how sperm cells are characterized can tell us a great deal about contemporary attitudes toward men.

Marveling at the capacities of sperm is a transhistorical phenomenon. In 2001, Bob Beale, an Australian science writer, illustrated the point with some sensational statistics:

> A normal healthy man makes as many as 1,500 sperm a second. That's 90,000 a minute; 5.4 million an hour; 130 million a day; almost 50 billion a year. At that rate, it would take no more than a fortnight for that one man to make a sperm for every fertile woman on the planet. The world's men produce up to 286,000,000,000,000,000 sperm a day: if you could stop the little blighters from wriggling and align them all end-to-end, the line would stretch for many millions of kilometers—enough to encircle the Equator thousands of times or to reach further than the Sun.[62]

Theories of sperm competition are not just produced in the laboratory; they also circulate in popular culture. Take, for example, the documentary *Enron: The Smartest Guys in the Room*, which chronicles the demise of the seventh-largest U.S. company into bankruptcy. Driven by the arrogance and greed of executives and the rapacity of Enron energy traders, the film illustrates the corporate culture created by chief executive officer Jeff Skilling—one of intense masculine exhibitions (corporate retreats with mandatory motorcycle races on treacherous terrain) and bare-knuckled competition. As a means to dramatize the competitive environment of Skilling's design, the filmmakers employ cutaways to imagery of sperm magnified under microscopes. By his own admission, Skilling's favorite book, *The Selfish Gene,* influenced his belief that macho competition was predestined based on the winning quality of the genes (the sperm) that form a person.[63]

Journalists are also engaged in their own sperm competition musings. In *Standup Guy: Masculinity That Works,* Michael Segell, a journalist for *Esquire* magazine, studied male behavior through focus groups, which he calls "bitchfests" and "cocktalks." He discusses the idea of sexual payback, whereby men bring women to climax and then do not go through with the sex act "all the way." "The only thing that's more enjoyable than having sex," one commodities trader explained to Segell, "is making a girl want it and not giving it to her."[64] Concerned with the difficulties of the dating scene for men and women ages 25–44, Segell guides men to return to a "new alpha male," a combination of traditional masculine qualities with emotional sensitivity, as a means to restore a certain type of social order in the dating world and hence reproduction. What are the connections, if any, between the new alpha male and the egg-getter, blocker, and seek-and-destroy sperm?

Segell uses Baker and Bellis's sperm competition theory as a means of explaining the male instinct to "keep a tightly clamped lid on the female libido."[65] Rather matter of factly, Segell writes:

> Let's say your wife is out of town for a week on business with six male colleagues, all of whom make about ten times as much money as you. Even if you ejaculate every day she's away, you'll still release more spermatozoa when she returns to your eager, trembling arms than you did during any of the (presumable) emissions. You'll also begin to manufacture more sperm designed to compete with a rival's sperm whose sole function is to fertilize an egg. Scientists consider this a sophisticated psycho-physiological adaptation to your unavoidable lapse in mate monitoring—or, put another way, to your possessive and suspicious nature.[66]

Segell's book also discusses the changing notions of fatherhood as related to the idea of being a stand-up guy in today's culture. He tracks how fatherhood has gone through changes and speaks of an almost-renaissance of fatherhood in which stand-up men want to be better fathers than their own, even though there is an added threat of chosen single motherhood to eliminate fathers.

In *The Decline of Males*, Lionel Tiger, an anthropologist who coined the term "male bonding" in the 1960s and argued that sexism was an evolutionary adaptation in the 1970s, explores how the birth control pill, women's role in the labor market, abortion, reproductive technology, and single motherhood have cut men out of reproduction:

> This book is about an emerging pattern. Men and women may not discern it clearly, but the pattern underlies their experiences in industrial society. It is the pattern of growth in the confidence and power of women and the erosion in the confidence and power of men. More women are having children without men, and therefore more men are without the love of families.[67]

According to Tiger, maleness and masculinity are not produced or constructed within the culture but are inherent or inborn variables that are threatened by women's ascendancy. This ascendancy is demonstrated by women's reproductive "choices," so that single motherhood is a threat to a man's ability to achieve love, connection, self-esteem, and well-being. In an article in the *New York Times* promoting the book, Tiger asserts:

> Men have been alienated from the means of reproduction. They don't feel they're rewarded enough by being family men, and there's no longer the coercion of religion or the law to discipline and motivate them. We won't solve the problem if we keep pretending that there's no difference between the sexes or shouting at men to behave more like women. We need new rules based on an understanding of the old rules of nature.[68]

It is not surprising that Tiger cites in laudatory fashion the work of Baker and Bellis as evidence that men change their sperm production and sperm's behavior to respond to these troubling sociocultural changes in women's contraceptive use and in participation in the labor force. Tiger also links what he sees as increases in extreme forms of masculine expression—"interest in sports and pornography"—as outlets for masculinity to be expressed when men "feel otherwise obligated to repress their masculinity."[69]

Scientists, journalists, doctors, and academics are just some of the participants in the process of asserting new gender rules or at least recasting rules of previous generations. North American men's movements have been characterized by some as driven by nostalgia for a previous image of the heteronormative, male-dominated nuclear family. Unfortunately, as depicted in some reactions to sperm science and spermatic commerce, many familial representations are taken as a version of a singular truth about biology and destiny. We must remember that these are not arbitrarily produced representations, and we must work to reinsert social analyses of the belief systems that these images recreate and perpetuate.

FLUID TENACITY

Despite ongoing changes regarding the access to and means of human reproduction, sperm and semen maintain definitions of tenacity, strength, and supremacy. Much like the fluid of semen itself can leak onto different fabrics and into different bodies, the meanings of semen are able to seep into our consciousness, transmitting the validity of stereotypically conservative views of men and women.

For centuries, scientists and scholars have attempted to define, manipulate, and control semen and sperm. Their work has been consistently informed and influenced by their own gendered and cultural understandings of men and masculinity and at times has even been a direct response to various crises in masculinity. As discussed in this chapter, the current historical moment is rife with examples of this practice. The scientific practices that elevate sperm to the lofty heights of sole reproductive actor also, ironically, transform sperm into a relatively easily accessible commodity. Modern reproductive technologies and services can now limit a man's role in human reproduction to that of an anonymous sperm donor. Certain men and women react to this spermatic marketplace by intensifying efforts to defend against what they perceive as an attack on masculinity and fatherhood.

Through a backlash against feminism, a battle cry has been issued to the ranks of men to stand up and defend their reign over the family. Thus, these sperm theories can provide a biological basis for responding to the contemporary crisis of masculinity. Men and women have answered the call—in the form of fathers' rights movements, policy recommendations about access to sperm banks, and the proliferation of human sperm competition research. What better icon to represent the struggle of real men at times of social upheaval than a kamikaze sperm, risking his life to enable the egg-getter sperm access to the egg? Sperm can go down in a blaze of glory as they retain their preeminence as the provider, protector, and rightful dominator of the family. It is not surprising that theories of sperm competition in all their popular and scientific permutations rely on notions of nostalgic forms of masculinity and stereotypical macho men. It is troubling, however, that different scholars and laypeople use this "scientific" theory as a means to further the agendas of certain types of oppressive or regressive family structures.

Consumers of scientific knowledge must ask how sperm and semen are understood, especially considering the intended and unintended assumptions about gender that theories about sperm and semen can produce. I would argue that the competitive images and representations of sperm are meant, sometimes unintentionally, to instruct or incite actual men and women. Thus, there is traffic between the ideal type of masculinity and the embodied performance of "being masculine" as exhibited by sperm and semen. At the same time, the meaning of masculinity is not concrete, consistent, and fixed; rather, since we all participate in ongoing interactions that define ideas about masculinity and femininity, this process is fluid and changes depending on historical and cultural circumstances. Still, as women have gained increasingly greater access and control to sperm without needing male approval or even an actual male, the rise of such hypermasculine imagery in regard to sperm cannot be underestimated as a form of male backlash.

3

My Sperm in Shining Armor

Children's Books

I began this book by detailing my own childhood recollection of being shown a facts of life book by my mother. As a mother myself now, I can only imagine what my mother must have gone through before having this little chat with me. Unknown to me at the time, my mother had given a lot of thought and time in preparing for this talk. Talking about sex did not often happen in our household, nor is sex talk often that common elsewhere—particularly when children are around. Talking about sex does not come easily for most, with or without children present. (Perhaps this reason more than any other explains the phenomenal success of the pornography industry, where the traffic of visual imagery, not words, is all that is really necessary.) Even finding that facts-of-life book had been a challenge, my mother tells me, as there were not many books of this kind readily available in upstate New York bookstores in the early 1970s. I can relate to, and especially appreciate, her anxiety. Since talking about sex isn't easy even between adults, talking to children about such a topic is even more difficult. And if that weren't enough, there are the comprehensive and conceptual differences between child-like and adult-like ways of thinking.

These reasons perhaps help explain why children's facts-of-life books are so steeped in euphemism and metaphors. The phrase "facts of life" alone is instructive. First, it is a euphemism: "facts" is a stand-in for the details of sexual intercourse, and "life" is an even more removed stand-in for conception. The word "facts" even suggests a clinical, cut-and-dried approach to this topic: "it's just the facts, kids, and they can't be avoided," parents might tell themselves. As such, the thinking goes, this talk is part of their parental duty to educate their children, however embarrassing these facts might be.

Such an approach also helps explain why, in looking at even very recent children's books, the story of conception is so narrowly presented. A man and a woman, overwhelmingly presumed to be husband and wife, or a male dog and a female dog or some other such animal pairing, have problem-free and desire-free (after all, this is not about sexual gratification) intercourse with his penis entering her vagina and his sperm releasing inside of her to journey to the egg.

These sex ed books are one of the ways in which cultural expectations are transmitted to children. Here, men, and by extension masculinity, are portrayed through illustrating the behavior of the sperm cell. Sperm is given a personality; it is often the hero. Just like in fairytales, age-appropriate descriptions of how sperm jostle to be the best mirrors the idea of the singular prince in shining armor who will save the day. As this chapter demonstrates, children's books explain human reproduction in conventional terms that reproduce idealized images of family, sexuality, and children. By depicting sperm as knights in shining armor, or as football stars or other athletic heroes, while simultaneously characterizing sperm cells as actual men and good husbands and fathers, children's books instruct children in what it means to be a good man.

In a way, one of the first sex manuals written for children in the English language was just that: an instruction book on how to be a good man. In 1915, Mary Ware Dennett (1872–1947), a suffragette and peace activist, researched and wrote a sex education manual for her adolescent sons (ages 11 and 15).[1] Because it was so popular among her sons and their peers, in 1919 Dennett self-published her "manual" as a pamphlet, *The Sex Side of Life: An Explanation for Young People*.[2] Dennett, as a single mother, wanted to maintain open communication with her sons regarding sex: "Remember to save all your questions and ask me. I will tell you *everything*. I don't want you to be able to grow up and say, 'Why didn't my mother tell me these things!'"[3] In her manual, sperm is described as the "male part of the germ of life," and ejaculation or "seminal emissions" are treated without judgment. She explains: "The spermatozoa are very tiny and the testicles hold many millions of them. Under the microscope they show a head and tail like a long pollywog. They become very active when released from the testicles and move by a rapid wriggling of the tail part."[4]

Under the claim of needing to protect the young from "bad influences," public and governmental reactions to children's books about sex were, and continue to be, fraught with controversy. The controversy surrounding publication of Dennett's pamphlet demonstrates a deeply rooted cultural ambivalence about teaching children about sex. Shortly after its initial publication, in 1922 the U.S. Postal System banned the distribution of Dennett's pamphlet as obscene.[5] Dennett, an activist at heart, was not deterred and pursued her cause in the landmark case of *The United States v. Dennett.* One of the most significant censorship cases in U.S. history, it ultimately transformed the legal definition of obscenity. The U.S. Court of Appeals for the Second Circuit reversed Dennett's obscenity conviction in 1930. This ruling took into account a publisher's intent when evaluating whether the literature was obscene.

More than 40 years after Dennett's case, Dorothy Broderick, a librarian and cofounder of *Voice of Youth Advocates,* summed up the purpose of children's facts of life books in her 1978 article, "Sex Education: Books for Young Children":

> Sex Education books should impart accurate information and healthy attitudes. Two essential attitudes must come through loud and clear: (1) the sexual act that leads to a baby being created should be connected with human emotions of loving and tenderness the man and woman feel for each other and make clear the commitment they have to each other and (2) the book should convey that having a baby is a conscious decision on the part of the couple and not an inevitability of the sex act.[6]

Broderick was famous for stating that every library in the country ought to have a sign on the door, reading: "This library has something offensive to everyone. If you are not offended by something we own, please complain." Although heroic in her fight against the repressive and omnipresent threat of censorship, these "essential attitudes" about the sex act have, over time, become the only attitudes—or the only permissible—story about reproduction that now gets told in children's books.

The problem, of course, is that many babies are made without planning, without love, without conventionally committed parents, and without a man and a woman actually present during fertilization. Conversely, in the case of surrogacy, there might be two mothers and a father present; in the case of test tube babies, no "actual" parents may be present at all, only lab technicians. Children who enter the world this way could be misled, confused, or ashamed by reading a book that does not reflect the reality of their conception. Further, the ideology embedded in the prescription for explaining sexual relations to children is also problematic. The couples are heterosexual, often depicted as married and engaging in sex purely for the purpose of conception, suggesting that only heterosexuals can become parents and that sex is a practical venture, with little pleasure involved.

The ubiquitous presence of heterosexuality establishes that children's books are engaging in what sexuality scholars would call the cementing of "heteronormativity." By "heteronormative" I mean the processes by which heterosexual relations (that is, genitally born boys who become men having sex with genitally born girls who become women) are produced as natural and reinforced as transparent and unambiguous notions. Heteronomativity is a powerful idea that shapes human behavior in that the concept refines and reproduces itself using social and cultural ideas to convince individuals of the inherent naturalness and thus superiority of heterosexuality.

THE CHILD'S WORLD

Children's culture is both a fantastic and a dangerous space to explore how sperm is represented. As historian Henry Jenkins has noted, "When we want to prove that something is so basic to human nature that it cannot be changed, we point to its presence in our children."[7] Children are often constructed as some form of presocialized creature that exist as biological beings and thus remain unmediated, animalistic, primitive, and naïve. The truth of human nature is often thought to be embodied in children. And we often lament that as our children mature, social forces "corrupt" them.

In an interesting parallel, sperm is also viewed as a presocialized biological entity that remains unmediated, animalistic, primitive, and naïve. Even though human reproduction is a complicated relationship that requires seemingly endless social negotiation, it is also assumed to be an innate biological drive that furthers the progress of human evolution. To erase this complex negotiation, we point to the presence of heterosexual and reproductive desires within our children. The naïve child's body, similar to the imagined sperm cell, is thought to be "naturally" heterosexual, monogamous, reproductive, and gender-specific. Such renderings remind us of one way that children first become socialized into the codes of sexual and gender behavior.

In my reading of facts-of-life books, I see an implied child's sexuality being presented, one that will naturally unfold as the outcome of a journey. Children are expected to react in certain ways and, with time, they probably will. The complication, of course, is the notion of these certain ways. As literary critic Jacqueline Rose points out, adults often panic that children's sexuality will be radically different from what's considered normal—normal being heterosexual and nondeviant.[8] As my research shows, with almost universal conformity, children's books present sex and conception as between a man and a woman and the act itself as not kinky. But though these books merely represent humans and animals as "normal" sexual beings (actually asexual sexual beings), they also use fantasy and fairy tale tropes to personify sperm as a compelling protagonist.

In *The Uses of Enchantment*, the Austrian-born American child psychologist Bruno Bettelheim explores the creation, dissemination, and consumption of fairy tales as processes of socialization.[9] To read fairy tales to children is to transmit role models in preparation for social rituals, most importantly heterosexuality. But children's literature does more than transmit certain cultural norms. Sociological and historical analyses of many texts have revealed persistent and pejorative representations of subordination, inferiority, weakness, and stupidity for those who rank low on the social ladder. Gender, racial or ethnic, age, and ability biases have been embedded in children's literature since the beginning of the genre.[10] Sex- and gender-role stereotyping is perhaps the most prevalent form of discrimination in preschool children's books.[11] Unraveling how gender-specific socialization and subsequent discrimination occurs through the consumption of children's culture helps us see how we regulate children to become good little girls and boys.

Bronwyn Davies, a sociologist of education, has produced some of the most important understandings of children's play, speech, and reading practices. Davies argues that in order for boys and girls to meet the social expectations that regulate their behavior, children must learn multiple "rules" about their gendered behavior. Being immersed in the culture, saturated with media (books, comics, TV, DVDs, the internet), and regulated by gendered sanctions such as teasing boys who watch princess movies, children learn what it means to give a "correct" gender performance.[12] Of course, children are not merely passive receptacles of information, they are also meaning-making beings and may interpret things differently than adults intend them to. In facts-of-life books, a child might be able to internally challenge some of the social expectations that are transmitted in the pages. However, children's ability to construct an alternate "reading" of a text is complicated by their self-reported practice of "adopt[ing] discourses simply in order to please teachers" and other adults.[13] Identifying with the hero of the story or having empathy for the heroine is often what guides a child's reading of a text. As sperm are overwhelmingly depicted as the heroes who must overcome tremendous obstacles in order to become "the one," children are placed in the position of rooting for the sperm cell.

Unlike self-identified fairy tales, which are clearly fictionalized and fantastic, children's facts-of-life books make many scientific claims. Perhaps in maintaining a fairy tale motif, children's books can ease into science, a marker of maturity, while at the same time preserving a notion of the precious innocence of childhood. There is a profound assertion in these books of the preeminence and "naturalness" of reproductive development and participation. These books also communicate norms, warnings, and rewards about human reproduction to children, usually aged 4–12, that are likely to have a lasting effect for many years. These books are morality tales with protagonist heroes, damsels, and villains culminating in a happily-ever-after ending.

One of the significant contributions of Davies's studies is her exploration of the difficulty of using an adult understanding of the world to interpret a child's understanding. "Meanings which seemed to me to be readily available to any listener were not necessarily readily available to [children],"[14] Davies points out. Because I am no longer a child, I do not know how a child now sees the world—other than my own memories of childhood and perhaps peripherally as a mother. As another professor of education, David Buckingham, articulates,

> Interpreting any children's program, and perhaps particularly one aimed at a very young audience, is fraught with difficulties. As adults, we are not the intended audience; and as such, there is a significant risk of "misreading," taking things too literally, or simply lapsing into pretentiousness. It is all too easy to dismiss such programs as boring or simplistic, or alternatively to find them cute or anarchic or surreal-

istic, responses which could be seen as characteristics of how adults relate to children generally. The danger here is that we end up simply imposing adult categories, and thereby making unwarranted assumptions about viewers. Spotting the intertextual references and symbolic associations or alternatively "hunting the stereotypes" are easy games to play; but they tell us very little about how children themselves interpret and relate to what they watch.[15]

That said, what I am offering here is a reading of children's books, which are written by adults, with an eye toward understanding what these children are expected to glean from these books. In this way, children's books, perhaps more so than other texts, offer us a polysemous read.

Before I begin my analysis of these children's books, it is important to note that contemporary reproductive endocrinology is largely taken as the default knowledge for these "child-appropriate" texts. By and large, these children's books are about human reproduction, written in response to the question, "Where did I come from?" To answer this question, most books also explore, to varying degrees of detail, heterosexual intercourse. Scientific explanations of human reproduction are similar to fairy tales in that they rely heavily on both symbolism and metaphor. These children's books also draw from discoveries in biology, anatomy, gynecology, and urology. When labeling and narrating reproductive processes, authors and illustrators use scientific terminology such as sperm, egg, ovum, and conception. Furthermore, the images, whether rendered through photography, drawing, or painting, are mediated by the use of scientific technologies such as electron microscopes, dissection, and x-rays. By relying on science, these children's books bolster their contents as being objective and truthful.

Based on the scientific synopsis of sperm from chapter 2, and given the great range of variability of sperm's shape and functionality, the discussion now can turn to the accuracy of representations of sperm in these children's books. A careful analysis shows that they take liberty with both "truth" and objectivity. Indeed, what is remarkable about the books that I examined is the conformity of social messages they offer and the "scientific" uniformity of what it means to be a normal sperm cell as reiterated through the child-appropriate scientific lens. For the purposes of this study, I analyzed 27 children's books, published over a 50-year span.[16] The books chosen for this examination were all written in the English language, represented sperm through narrative or visual images, were text-based, and had an intended audience of children aged 4–12. The publication dates spanned between 1952 and 2001.

In the following analysis, I build a theory about the transference that occurs between humans and cells, specifically men and sperm. I also develop a nascent theory about the interconnectedness of disembodiment and anthropomorphism. I use the term "anthropomorphism" to mean the act of attributing human forms or qualities to entities that are not human or have not attained "personhood." Children's book authors anthropomorphize nearly everything, from letters of the alphabet to cats in hats to the Berenstain bears. Like the characters in other children's books, sperm and egg cells are described in facts-of-life books as having human form and expressing human emotions such as jealousy, competition, or love. This anthropomorphism of sperm and eggs offers a way for sperm or eggs to dance their way into children's imaginations.

THE BIRDS AND THE BEES

In the world of children's books, humans are placed in a biological continuum with flowers, amphibians, and mammals. Many books precede the discussion of human reproduction with an exploration of nature and hence "natural" relationships. Other species, such as flowers, birds, bees, and dogs are shown as all "fitting together"—a description used in several books as a way to indicate the predetermined way that "beings" intuit how to reproduce. *How Babies Are Made,* published in 1968, shows animals in different sexual reproductive positions such as "doggie-style." First there are the chickens, then the dogs, and, with the final illustration in the natural continuum, humans. Universally, these books present idealized images of humans and human biology with no imperfections. Not surprisingly, there are virtually no images or discussion of infertility, assisted reproductive technologies (ARTs), alternative family configurations, or the existence of sexual desire and gratification for its own sake.

In many children's books, the first few pages are about the courtship and performance of all species. In the kindergarten-to-sixth-grade book, *First Comes Love: All About the Birds and Bees—and Alligators, Possums and People, Too,* for instance, jaunty rhyme and comedic illus-

Figure 3.1. Sperm and egg cells, like men's and women's bodies, fit together. From Jennifer Davis, *First Comes Love: All About the Birds and the Bees—and Alligators, Possums and People, Too*, 2001.

trations are used to discuss courtship, mating, and birth: "Love starts as a twinkle in two people's eyes, warming the hearts of both gals and guys. Animals, too, feel this wild attraction; it makes the males spring into action. Once they've picked a special sweetheart, then dazzling displays of affection start."[17] After enacting some natural role of performance, like bringing flowers or fending off a competing male, the new animal couple intuitively find a way to "fit together," culminating in a baby being made and born (figure 3.1).

In the end the perfect baby is on a pedestal with a cheering, delighted audience (figure 3.2). This is the grand finale, where the baby is the epitome of achievement for the two parents. The treatment of a child's birth as an achievement, albeit natural, is echoed in many children's books. Perhaps this achievement is supposed to make the child reader feel good, as if they've achieved something remarkable already just by being born.

Figure 3.2. Babies are prizes or accomplishments resulting from the impressive feats of competitive sperm cells. From Jennifer Davis, *First Comes Love: All About the Birds and the Bees—and Alligators, Possums and People, Too,* 2001.

SETTING THE MOOD

Since sex is often talked about euphemistically and through metaphors, one common technique in sex ed books is to begin by setting the mood using comparisons with flowers. Flowers, unlike animals, are presented without having to be anthropomorphized. Flowers differ from animals because animals have feelings, and so do humans (and as we'll see, so do sperm cells). Such books work to set the ambience or the context under which reproduction should occur—foreplay, if you will. Most important is the emotional context in which heterosexual, properly gendered humans are shown to be in love and in a committed, monogamous relationship (there is no question of paternity). These are intentional actors guided by their intense feelings for one another and the "beauty" of their physical contact. They have the appropriate anatomical equipment. They have potent and fertile bodies, most often white-skinned, that fit together, particularly in the missionary position (unlike animals). Finally, these humans always perform their sex acts at home and in a bed (often decoratively detailed in pastels with soft brush strokes or humorous cartoons).

Peter Mayle, a pioneer of the children's sex ed book (and subsequent author of the *My Year in Provence* series), published *Where Did I Come From? The Facts of Life Without Any Nonsense and with Illustrations* in 1977. This book earned respect and a warning from famed child expert Dr. Benjamin Spock, who said, "I give this book top grades for humanness and honesty. Some parents will find that its humourousness helps them over the embarrassment. Others may be offended."

Mayle's book, written for 5–10 year olds, famously depicts a sperm in a tuxedo that is referred to as "the romantic sperm." The caption reads: "How could an egg resist a sperm like this?" (figure 3.3). This exceptional anthropomorphized sperm cell clearly indicates the contexts of human reproduction. First is the emotional context: the romantic

How could an egg resist a sperm like this?

Figure 3.3. Romantic and irresistible sperm as anthropomorphized with top hat and tail. From Peter Mayle, *Where Did I Come From? The Facts of Life Without Any Nonsense and with Illustrations*, 1977.

sperm sits on a heart, blushing and smiling in a suggestive fashion; second is the physical context: it has senses (eyes, nose, mouth, hands); and third is the material context: it is classy and cultured with a top hat, bow tie, and "tails." The sperm cell becomes a character children can root for in the pursuit of its goals and desires.[18]

There is also a concomitant moral tale of the specialness of the sex act, a personal and intimate connection not to be shared with just anyone. Weddings are illustrated in several books. Among them are *The Birds and the Bees,* for 9–12 year olds; *The Wonderful Way Babies Are Made,* a Christian book for 4–8 year olds; *Who Am I? Where Did I Come From?* (figure 3.4), Dr. Ruth's book for 4–8 year olds; *Where Do Babies Come From? A Series for the Christian Family,* for 6–8 year olds; and *Wonderfully Made,* a Lutheran book for 10–12 year olds. Transference between sperm and egg cells and human beings is also evident in these books. Just as the man and woman are in love, so are sperm and egg. The emotions and actions of the human reproducers are transferred to their replacements—the sperm and egg traveling inside their bodies.

These cells become the stand-ins for the mom and dad since sperm and eggs are appropriately gendered. Sperm is depicted as blue, and eggs are colored pink. Sperm are identified as "him" and "his." Furthermore, when sperm speak to one another, they use male terms to achieve male bonding: "Come on, boys!" In the book for 4–8 year olds, *Where Willy Went,* the first book to feature a sperm cell as the main character, Willy is taunted by a competitor sperm cell, Butch. "Call that swimming?" Butch says as he menacingly pursues Willy during his practice laps. But Willy prevails because "he was the BEST at swimming! HURRAH!" (figure 3.5). In many books, eggs are also gendered with false eyelashes, perfume, makeup, and hearts—however they rarely have any speaking lines (figure 3.6).

The majority of the books disembody the action by placing the site of reproduction in a centralized place, often circled or separated out from the rest of the body. Disembodiment is the process whereby body parts, fluids, and organs are removed from their physical and somatic contexts and viewed as independent of the human forms from which they come. The uterus and penis are both unencumbered by the complexity and messiness of the human body (and psyche and desire) from which they emerge. They are presented as independent parts, functioning as closed systems, centralized only in the penis and uterus.

When boys and girls grow up, they become adults. And when adults love each other very much, they get married. At some point, the grown-ups might decide to try to get pregnant and have a baby.

So, the man puts his penis inside the woman's vagina. This is called having sex.

There are two important things you should know about making love. It feels very good, and mommies and daddies only do it in **private**, when they are alone.

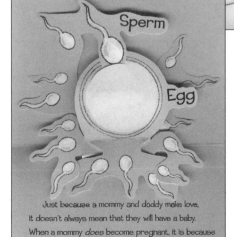

Sperm

Egg

Just because a mommy and daddy make love, it doesn't always mean that they will have a baby. When a mommy *does* become pregnant, it is because sperm from the daddy's penis came together with the egg, which is inside the mommy.

Figure 3.4. In the style of a pop-up book, the illustrations depict a sequence of events: first a wedding; then the married couple in bed; and then, when you open the flap, sperm are circulating in the egg. From Dr. Ruth K. Westheimer, *Who Am I? Where Did I Come From?*, 2001.

Figure 3.5. The first book of its kind to focus on a sperm cell as the main character celebrates the victory of Willy. From Nicholas Allan, *Where Willy Went*, 2004.

Maps with detailed directions and highlighted pathways of sperm reproduction teach readers about the sperm's journeys (figure 3.7). The journey is illustrated with names of places, directions, and legends. Notably, body parts are not anthropomorphized but treated as an objective "environment" for the egg and sperm. The children's books' imagery and text switch back and forth from the disembodiment of human body parts to anthropomorphizing the sperm and egg where cells are given human attributes, personalities, and scripts. Kids are asked to switch identification from the human parents, seeing the sperm as the knight and the egg as the damsel.

It's So Amazing: A Book About Eggs, Sperm, Birth, Babies, and Families, for children 7 and up, uses a comic book motif to follow a bird and bee through their education about sex and sexuality. This book, perhaps the most progressive of my sample, includes discussions of adoption and gay and lesbian parenting. In this book and a few others, the site of reproduction also provides a context for capitalist principles of production and competition. In this way, the book naturalizes

Figure 3.6. Egg cells wait for sperm cells to win them in the reproductive race. From Jennifer Davis, *First Comes Love: All About the Birds and the Bees—and Alligators, Possums and People, Too*, 2001.

Figure 3.7. Maps that illustrate the human reproductive anatomy are prevalent in many children's books. From Laurie Krasny Brown and Marc Brown, *What's the Big Secret? Talking About Sex with Girls and Boys*, 1997.

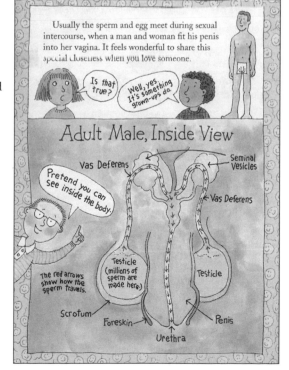

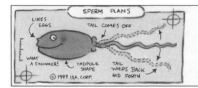

Sperm are shaped like tadpoles. Their long tails are what make them such speedy swimmers. When scientists watch sperm swim under a microscope, they can actually see the sperm's tails whipping and lashing back and forth.

Figure 3.8. In a blueprint format of "sperm plans," children are introduced to variables that make up a sperm cell. From Robie Harris, *It's So Amazing: A Book About Eggs, Sperm, Birth, Babies and Families,* 1999.

the processes of capitalism. The industrial imagery of a seminal assembly line likens sperm production to the factory production line. Maps and directions offer more precision for the factory to mass-produce the best sperm. The man's body itself is a factory of mass production whose purpose is the further production of labor power. There is even a blueprint for factory production of the quintessential sperm, complete with smiling face and tail in motion (figure 3.8). This image of the assembly line entitled "sperm plans" provides measurements of sperm and evaluative comments such as "What a swimmer!" and "Likes eggs."[19] This is further illustrated by a drawing of the male reproductive system with colored arrows that show how the sperm travels. Echoing the fast food assembly line, testicles are labeled with "millions of sperm are made here." The sperm then race through the factory of complex machinery and fueling stations.

A competition metaphor is also used to show the sperm moving and talking about their feelings and actions. Getting there first is a theme in many books like *First Comes Love,* where there is a race to the finish line. Sperm also inform one another of their losses: "What's happening is we just lost the race" says one dud sperm to another as they turn to swim away from the victor.

In many books, a recurring theme suggests that the closer we get to the moment of conception, the more disembodied the human actors become. At this time, agency, personality, and subjectivity transfer from the human parents to their sperm and egg cells. It is as if the sperm and egg exclusively take over the action and conscious decision-making. The human parents are solely staging grounds for the gendered performances of these cells.

SWIMMING INTO ACTION

The claims of the historical legacy of sperm's and men's crucial, necessary, and even exclusive role in human reproduction have been well documented and analyzed.[20] Children's books play a key part in keeping this interpretation of sperm's centrality alive. Some of these texts echo theories of men starting life and not needing an egg, just a womb to incubate the fully formed miniature human contained in a single sperm cell. Historically, this representation of a man's sperm contains a homunculus, a tiny adult inhabiting a single cell, that will increase in size to form an adult human. In *Where Did I Come From?* "A spurt of quite thick, sticky stuff comes from the end of the man's penis and this goes into the woman's vagina. Well, believe it or not, this sticky stuff is how you and I and all of us started. It's called semen, and in the semen are sperm." (figure 3.9). Taking the representation of the egg as passive and mute one step farther, this text in effect erases women's biological participation in reproduction by not mentioning the egg at all.

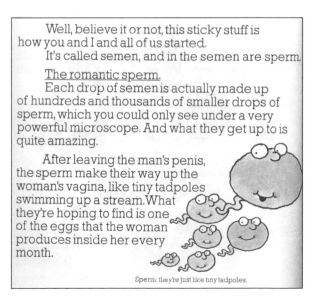

Figure 3.9. Tadpoles are consistently evoked when illustrating sperm in books. From Peter Mayle, *Where Did I Come From? The Facts of Life Without Any Nonsense and with Illustrations*, 1977.

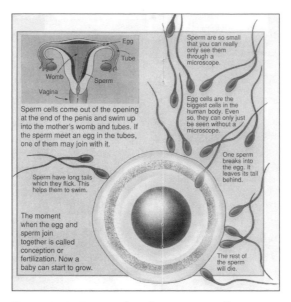

Figure 3.10. Images that show sperm cells entering into a sun-like egg are common. From Susan Meredith, *Where Do Babies Come From?*, 1991.

In many books, sperm are portrayed as having consciousness, self-reflexivity, and the ability to communicate with each other. Sperm are good workers, they are happy and willing to do what they are programmed to do, and they can learn through training and persistence—practice makes perfect, after all. Sperm are integral to insemination: the sperm cell is portrayed as having a purposeful goal and as being capable of intentional actions and autonomy. As discussed with the romantic sperm, sperm cells have feelings, too. Even when sperm are not anthropomorphized, the imagery is impressive, as in *Where Do Babies Come From?* This Christian book offers an image of sperm moving toward the big sunlight of the glowing egg (figure 3.10).

In *Growing Up: How We Become Alive, Are Born and Grow,* the author Karl de Schweinitz uses pen and ink drawings of 19 sperm circling around one large white circle. *A Kid's First Book About Sex* written by Joani Blank, a sex therapist, educator, and founder of Good Vibrations, a sex toy emporium, depicts images reminiscent of the Jedi knight (the small but defined sperm cell) racing toward the death star (the large black circle egg cell). Dr. Ruth's pop-up book illustrates sperm in three dimensions surrounding the egg from many angles. *First Comes Love* illustrates sperm racing to the finish line where an egg with a heart is waiting.

There is a preponderance of narratives describing the exceptionalness of the one sperm that gets to fertilize the egg. Other than primping and batting eyes to be attractive to the sperm, eggs typically are passive. In *First Comes Love,* the feminized egg appears dainty and fragile on a red tasseled pillow. Sperm are described with active verbs and in prototypically masculine terms like faster, swims, hurries, digs, wagging, fertilize, strong, healthy, wow, and yahoo. Eggs, in contrast, are described with passive verbs and feminine terms: waits, travels, beautiful, and is released. Eggs are described much less frequently than sperm, which brings to the fore the seemingly more important activity of the sperm cells.

Most books remind us that the father's sperm are even smaller than the egg—so small, you can see them only with a microscope. In most of the books, sperm from different animals are illustrated as having different shapes, but they always have heads and tails. The tail moves and helps the sperm swim quickly. There are outliers for these representations that stand out as significant. As a sign of the feminist movement or perhaps a commentary on recent innovations in reproductive endocrinology, *It's So Amazing* states, "Scientists have discovered that if an egg is in one of the tubes, a chemical in the liquid around the egg attracts one sperm out of the two hundred sperm— just like a magnet." However, unable to shake off the repressive context, this text is accompanied by an illustration of an egg, coiffed with lipstick and blush, putting on perfume (figure 3.11). A sperm attracted to the egg (we can tell because of the hearts in his text bubble) says to another sperm:

Figure 3.11. Sperm making their way to the coiffed egg. From Robie Harris, *It's So Amazing: A Book About Eggs, Sperm, Birth, Babies and Families,* 1999.

I feel a strange attraction.
What's around the corner?
See anything yet?
I feel like I'm being pulled by a magnet.
Oh my! Look at that!!

It's So Amazing is also unique in that the book incorporates assisted reproductive technologies into the storyline. When the sperm can't swim fast enough or otherwise don't perform, a scientist helps them function properly. Scientists have different roles in this book. First, the scientist is a matchmaker: "In fact, scientists have figured out several ways for an egg cell and a sperm cell to meet." Next, the scientist is God-like, or perhaps pimp-like, depending on your perspective: "Doctors can place sperm into the vagina or uterus with a syringe—a tube like an eyedropper. The sperm can then swim to the Fallopian tubes where a sperm can meet and join with an egg. Or doctors can put an egg and a sperm in a special laboratory dish where egg and sperm can meet and join together." And finally, the scientist is a club owner or swinging single: "There are times when a man and a woman have sexual inter-course, but do not wish to make a baby. Scientists have invented ways called 'birth control' that can keep a sperm and egg from meeting. And if a sperm and egg do not meet, the beginning cells of a baby cannot start to grow." As in unassisted reproduction, there is a certain continuity of erasing the active participation of women and eggs when scientists get involved.

"WE WAS ROBBED"

In children's books, not all sperm are created equal. Embedded in sperm imagery from cartoon books are smiling, competitive, or befud-dled sperm talking to one another and presumably the audience. These sperm evaluate themselves and others based on their ability to follow directions, swim quickly, navigate the difficult terrain, and eventually merge with the egg. In children's books, the measure of the better sperm is loosely based on motility, not morphology.

From a subset of the sample, secular books that anthropomorphize sperm, we learn that sperm have desire; sperm are in a race; sperm are competitive; among sperm, there will be only one winner; sperm have

Figure 3.12. The children teach the parents about sperm racing to eggs. From Babette Cole, *Mommy Laid an Egg: or, Where Do Babies Come From?*, 1993.

a sense of entitlement and fairness; sperm can be powerful; and speedy, active sperm are good, while fatigue and slowness are bad.

For example, In *Where Did I Come From?* Mayle states that "for most of the time, though, your sperm are inside your body, waiting and twiddling their thumbs. What they would really like to do is get out." In *Mommy Laid an Egg,* Babette Cole, British children's author and illustrator, uses the outrageous stupidity of the parents as a foil to instruct children about the facts of life (figure 3.12). Sperm are depicted with racing stripes and numbers on them, and they state "Gotcha" and "We was robbed" as they race en masse to the egg. There is also a sense of male bonding in that sperm cheer each other on. "Come on, boys" appears in a few books, including *How Are Babies Made?*, as a rallying cry from the masses of sperm in pursuit of the egg.

Present even in the books that do not explicitly anthropomorphize sperm is a quality of exceptionalness to the sperm that is able to swim and fertilize the egg. Out of the many millions of sperm that exist, the one that actually "swims" to join with the egg is important. I would argue that the recurring narrative of being "the one" fosters a sense of a male entitlement, encouraging egotism and an exaggerated feeling of being superior to all others. The distinction of being *the one* sperm that gets to inseminate the egg is represented almost universally in the books I analyzed. This biological narrative that encourages a superiority complex in boys might belie centuries of male inferiority and insecurity in reproduction and parenting. Hierarchies among men are also established along the way through the naturalization of competitions based on physical strength, endurance, and speed. To be "the one" is to be the best: to win.

"IT'S ALL GOD'S PLAN"

While reading these children's books, I was struck by both the similarities and the distinct differences between secular books and those that labeled themselves explicitly Christian. Similar to secular books, Christian books do maintain an integration of the biological continuum and an exclusively heterosexual context for human sexual relations. *Wonderfully Made*, Ruth Hummel's 1967 Lutheran book, states, "God wants only a husband and his wife to make love in this way. Husbands and wives have promised to live together always and to make a home for their children." Another by Ruth Hummel, *Where Do Babies Come From? A Series for the Christian Family*, presents images of God's plan of heterosexual coupling and matrimony that abound with imagery of weddings or brides and grooms. During a heart-to-heart mother and daughter conversation, Hummel writes,

> "Is that when they get married and they're a bride and groom and everything?"
>
> Suzanne put her ribbon on her hair and pretended it was a veil.
>
> "Yes, God is happy when two people decide to get married and start a life together with His blessing," Mother continued. "He made them for living together and showing their love to each other all their life. At special times they like to hold each other very close. God made their bodies so they fit together in a wonderful way.

"At those times the sperm from the man's body can go into the woman's body. Sometimes a sperm and an ovum join in the mother's body. That is when a baby begins."

Despite these similarities, a remarkable and striking difference begins to emerge—Christian books do not represent sperm in an anthropomorphized fashion. Rather, they are much more scientific than secular books. This Christian approach—by its avoidance of personifying sperm as an actual daddy—constructs heterosexuality as problem-free, just as much as the secular books do. There is no room for people who are unwilling or unable to have this kind of sex. In secular books, sperm and eggs are transformed into happy characters with smiling faces. The knowledge of social reproduction is transferred to the emotional and anthropomorphic sperm and egg. Readers are asked to identify with new protagonists of sperm and egg. This anthropomorphism is the crux of how children learn to identify with the good guy—the sperm, that is—the properly gendered male, who is happily mass-produced, a diligent laborer, heterosexual, and cheerfully competitive but a good sport, cocky, intentional, speedy: a winner.

Christian books do not require these characters (dressed or talking) because their values are prescribed by their faith. The intelligent designer, or God, is the most significant agent guiding human (and cellular) interaction. There is complete disembodiment during the site of reproduction, and the sperm is not anthropomorphized. Volition or purposeful action does not rest with the sperm, nor are the sperm and egg depicted as proxies for humans. Rather, agency is wholly relegated to God: "It's God's wonderful way," and, "Yes, that's the way God planned it! Both mother and father have a part in making the baby, but God has the biggest part."[21] In this way, there is no exchange of personality or will from man to sperm; God is the only actor in the story. Conception does not need to be taught through happy smiling tadpoles; it is transmitted through an all-knowing, omnipotent God. Sperm does not get ascribed with human achievements and failures. This reinforces a classic Christian interpretation of social problems: "love the sinner, hate the sin." That is, there are no bad people, just bad behaviors. In this case, the Christian view of sexual acts that are outside this framework as going against God's will becomes clear. The human embodiment is perfect because it comes from God; it is just the behavior that is wrong, whether it be homosexuality, promiscuity, or infidelity. By relegating the entire "natural order" to God, Christian children's books are able to code prescriptive social norms as God's will when describing human reproduction. God is all-knowing, guiding all normative human relations down to the miraculous creation of babies.

Christian books also universally establish that once the sperm enters the egg, a baby, with physical traits and a personality, is made. Christenson's *The Wonderful Way Babies Are Made* describes this being as "athletic, or musical or artistic or mechanical." Carolyn Nystrom's pastel-illustrated *Before I Was Born* explains that, after conception, "then the sperm joins the egg and they become one new cell no bigger than this dot. A baby is already being formed. If you could see inside that tiny cell, you could know whether the baby will have blue or brown eyes, whether it will have dark or light hair, whether it will be a boy or a girl, and even how tall it will be when it is all grown up."

Since Christian books do not invest sperm with personalities, God is the hero of each story. In *I Wonder, I Wonder,* the daddy responds to the children's curiosity about how babies grow by stating, "It's God's magic." And God is pleased with humans when they follow His specific plan for reproduction. In addition to using biblical texts throughout, the explanation of human reproduction in *My Body and Me: For Middle-Age Children* uses bold and all caps to summarize the information with "AND THAT IS GOOD!" at the end of each section. However, because Christian books do not address fertility, when a couple has trouble conceiving, one can only wonder whether God doesn't want them to conceive. To date, there has been no Christian children's sex ed book that addresses assisted reproductive technologies. But if the prevalence of ART increases, we can be fairly certain one will be produced soon.

In many ways, these Christian books present a simpler and more straightforward story of sperm's role in reproduction. The lack of complexity belies the strict moral regulation of human sexual interaction that supports the ideology of these texts. Since God is the hero—the omniscient one and the intelligent designer—God plans human interaction to occur in very particular ways. To some adults (and children), these stories might actually read more like fairy tales than secular books do.

Children's books about human reproduction attempt to explain biological processes to a young audience. However, they are also reproducing guidelines for how children should understand gender, sexual orientation, relationships, and even citizenship. Unfortunately, many of these representations are taken as a version of a singular truth about biology and destiny. We must remember that these are not arbitrarily produced representations but are carefully crafted to pass on conventional, even conservative, belief systems that, ultimately, the images and ideas presented in these books help to re-create and perpetuate.

SPERM OF TOMORROW

While *It's So Amazing* comes close to providing a more progressive option that expresses the range of variation of origin stories for children, this book, similar to all the others, still relies on age-old gender-based illustrations of sperm and eggs. More books are needed that depict variations of origin stories featuring adoption, single parenting, sperm donation, assisted reproductive technologies, and blended families. But more than that, an alternative method is needed to separate out the stereotypical gender roles that are inscribed into human reproductive cells.

My vision of this type of children's book would likely be one that discusses reproduction in the simplest terms possible. Something like: At this point in time, there are two options for human conception, sperm and egg cells can join inside a woman's body or they are merged in a laboratory setting and are then placed as an embryo into a woman's body. Although sperm does come from male bodies, sperm are not men; they are not gendered and not sentient beings with emotions and personalities. Furthermore, there are multiple ways to procure and disseminate sperm—through ejaculating penises or surgical techniques, by vaginal penetration, syringes, turkey basters, and catheters.

Stories matter, and stories we tell children are especially salient. Children's books are powerful as they are socialization in action. These books are not just "Where do babies come from?" But, "Who am I?" And "How did I get here?" And, "What kind of person am I?" Implicit in that answer is a whole host of assumptions about gender, sex, sexuality, marriage, and health that need to be considered. The larger point here is having "new" or other understandings of masculinity in order to expand the story of who we are. What if sperm were gendered as male and female? Or perhaps as Judith Lorber suggests, perhaps cultural representations of sperm could be completely "degendered."[22]

If sperm can be disentangled from men and masculinity, perhaps fatherhood can be expanded beyond paternity. There are distinct differences when considering what it is to father a child versus to mother a child. To father a child is to provide the sperm. The children's books play into this limited definition by making sperm such active, entertaining, and engrossing characters. It is as if your father did all his important work before you were even born. Mothering is another matter, and perhaps these representations of the egg are somehow related. Consider the oddity of thinking of mothering a child as just providing an egg. Ovum and mothering are rarely connected in such exclusive terms in the popular imaginary.

When our daughters ask us where they came from articulated in the question, "How did I get in Mommy's tummy?" I tell them that Mommy and Mom got some sperm from a friend, and Mom put it inside my vagina. The sperm and the fluid in my vagina then moved the sperm toward an egg. This sperm and egg joined to begin the process of creating you. This story has been told many times and changes as the girls age.

The matter-of-factness of this conception story has been quite empowering for my oldest daughter. During recess one year, a couple of first-grade boys approached my older daughter, Grace, to ask if she had a father. She said, "No, I have two moms." Apparently these boys found this to be impossible, walked over to the slide and told two other boys about Grace's claim. The four boys returned to Grace. They were incredulous and declared, "You have to have a dad. It doesn't make any sense." Grace, a particularly calm and thoughtful 6 year old, said, "Well, I don't. My moms have a friend who gave them sperm so I could be born." The boys, satisfied by this answer, then asked Grace if she wanted to play freeze tag and they continued on with recess.

4

Overcome

The Money Shot in Pornography and Prostitution

For a few years in the early 1990s, I worked on a national sex information switchboard. Much to my surprise, a majority of the callers were men, and their two most common questions were "What is the normal penis size?" and "Where is the clitoris?" Trained to provide anonymous, nonjudgmental, and accurate information to callers, I would respond that most penises, when erect, were between 5 and 7 inches. I would receive immediate thanks for this information, and as they hung up I remember thinking their relief was palpable. Their penises, presumably, were "okay."

As for the clitoris question, I instructed callers to place their hands in a praying position, bend their knuckles slightly and imagine this as the vagina. If the area between the thumbs was the vagina opening, the clitoris was roughly located in the place above the tips of their thumbs, in the triangular area. This answer was not as successful as the first. Many callers fumbled with or even dropped the phone while trying to follow my instructions. Some callers were clearly confused by the model itself, asking, "So it's a hole?" or "But what does the vagina really look like?" Furthermore, I was increasingly alarmed by the steady stream of female callers who asked for instructions on how to find their own clitorises or, somewhat paradoxically, wanted suggestions on how to experience orgasms exclusively though vaginal penetration. "Is there something wrong with me?" they inquired when discussing their dissatisfaction with penis-vagina penetration, often explaining that they had never experienced an orgasm during sex. Clearly, there is something baffling and mysterious about the clitoris. Even though size doesn't matter, location and purpose do. Where is it? What does it do? These callers rarely hung up with the same sense of relief as the first set of callers. The former found answers; the latter continued to question.

I use these examples to illustrate the conventional wisdom on male and female anatomy and sexual responses. In contrast to women, and whether or not each man experiences it to be true, conventional wisdom holds that men's sexuality is fairly simple. It isn't difficult to make men come, and it isn't difficult to know whether or not they have come. The phenomenon of men faking orgasm, though possible, doesn't often get discussed. Semen is, of course, the reason for this; it is thought to be the irrefutable evidence.

Although male callers rarely asked about their semen, in our training, we were instructed to provide them with these facts. Spermatogenesis, or the production of the sperm cell, takes approximately 72 days. Both Cowper's and Littre's glands, which are located in the genital area, contribute secretions in the processes of ejaculation. The prostate also adds fructose and liquefying enzymes.[1] When a man comes, a range of 2–10 milliliters of fluid is produced though his ejaculation at about 10 miles per hour. Between 200 and 500 million sperm cells are contained in most ejaculates, the equivalent of about 5–15 calories. It is estimated that a man ejaculates 5,000 times in his lifetime.[2] Theoretically any man could repopulate the United States with just a few ejaculates (and the participation of 290 million women or less if multiple births occur).

GROWING UP: FROM INNOCENCE TO DEBAUCHERY

In chapter 3, I explore how children's books both literally and symbolically sanitize semen.[3] In reading these books to children, we transmit the information that sperm cells are friendly and purposeful and that they diligently work to make mommy pregnant. For the most part, risk, danger, and sexual pleasure are not discussed or illustrated. But as children grow, they are bombarded by other ideas and images of sperm from media and popular culture. From exploding beer bottles on freeway billboards to public service announcements about condoms and safer sex, very different messages, metaphors, and images of sperm and semen soon materialize. These images tend to emphasize either the dangers or the pleasures of ejaculate.

Ejaculation is taken as external proof that a man has experienced an orgasm, despite evidence that men can ejaculate without orgasm, technically known as anorgasmic ejaculation.[4] The physical presence of the ejaculate, the seminal fluid, is a material reality that confirms men's pleasure.[5] Most pornographic entertainment reinforces this belief, as ejaculation, or the "money shot" in porn parlance, is the raison d'être of sexual encounters.[6] The money shot signals the end of the male sexual act—cue the drum roll, he has come. Cindy Patton, an activist and scholar of human sexuality, points out that in Western culture male sexual fulfillment is "synonymous with orgasm" and that the male orgasm is "an essential and essentialist punctuation of the sexual narrative. No orgasm, no sexual pleasure. No cum shot, no narrative closure."[7] In other words, the cum shot is the period at the end of the sentence. Case closed. Alternatively, with the rare exception of anorgasmic ejaculation, both the female anatomy and orgasm are more complex, even elusive— for both men and women. That being the case, in pornography the sex act itself is centered around the male penis and orgasm. Only when that happens does conventional wisdom tell us that sex has occurred.[8]

There is an entire lexicon for the release of semen from the body, terms like ejaculation, premature ejaculation, nocturnal emissions, wet dreams, and shooting your wad are just a few. With such a wide variety of ways to describe ejaculates and the act of ejaculating, it would seem that many men are preoccupied with ejaculation, and especially measurements of it. From the record books to website legends, claims about the feats of men and their ejaculations abound. For example, the world record for number of male orgasms is 16 in one hour. According to several unsubstantiated reports on websites, the greatest distance of an ejaculate is 18 feet 9 inches, which was achieved by Horst Schultz, who apparently also holds the record for the greatest height of ejaculate (12 feet 4 inches).

Not all ejaculates are created equal. Each time ejaculation occurs, semen contains varying proportions of ingredients. These variations are affected by diet, age, how the ejaculation was achieved (through masturbation or partner sexual stimulation, whether anal, oral, or vaginal), level of arousal, physical fitness, and number of ejaculations in the past 72 hours. The age of first conscious ejaculation, known as "oigarche," is generally between 10 and 15 years old. Nocturnal emissions, or wet dreams that are generally erotic or sexual, are accompanied by the release or ejaculation of semen. Roughly 50 percent of boys between the ages of 10 and 20 experience wet dreams, possibly as a way for the reproductive system to get rid of excess semen, although most agree that semen is reabsorbed back into the body.

But sometimes men are not physiologically in control of when and how their semen emerges. Premature ejaculation, recently renamed "rapid ejaculation" (in a similarly euphemistic twist as "impotence" which has been redubbed "erectile dysfunction") is increasingly considered a medically diagnosable condition for men under 40. It is defined as ejaculation prior to the desires of both sexual partners. Although rapid ejaculation may be underreported, the National Health and Social Life Survey suggests that its prevalence is roughly 30 percent. Sex therapy, antidepressants, and lidocaine cream or related topical anesthetic agents have all demonstrated success at treating rapid ejaculation.

Regardless of the quantity of semen or the quality of its delivery during ejaculation, in the world of sex entertainment the release of semen signifies the successful conclusion of the sex act. The appearance of semen is the proof of sexual fulfillment, so the more the more better, right? It turns out that the equation is not so simple when we consider the layered meanings of sperm and semen across the worlds of pornography, prostitution, and popular culture.

FETISHIZING SEMEN

Members of the specifically heterosexual[9] sex entertainment industry, sex workers and pornographic filmmakers in particular, contribute to our understanding of sperm in important ways. From ideas about what constitutes sex or sex acts to what is considered sexy, to how men and their penises can perform, the sex industry—even if covertly—has greatly influenced popular notions of sex. Pornographic filmmakers specialize in representing a variety of techniques to animate ejaculation and semen, thereby fetishizing it. Within sex entertainment settings, semen is worshiped as a magical substance of both supernatural arousal and erotic achievement. It is depicted in films and printed media as a substance that has extraordinary power over humans. The male actors seem repeatedly shocked by the force, volume, and desirability of their semen, while the female actors can't control themselves in the presence of this semen and must slather it all over their bodies, even drink it down as if dying of thirst. Different cultures vary the themes of seminal ejaculate in their pornography. For example, in the late 1990s, *bukkake*, a style of pornography that was popularized in Japan, depicts multiple men ejaculating on a woman or group of women.[10] The use of ejaculation is part of a humiliation ritual and generally does not involve any of the female characters experiencing orgasm.

So although semen is presented as the end product of a sexual experience, it is also an object manipulated by the directors, cameras, lighting, scripts, and actors to elicit arousal. The camera lens focuses on the glory of seminal expression and encourages the viewer to witness the money shot as the reward of spectatorship. The framing of the money shot is perhaps the most sincere devotion to and idolization of semen that I've encountered.

But semen does not exist in a vacuum; rather, it is a bodily fluid that is deeply implicated in history and epidemiology. At least for the past 30 years, unprotected seminal ejaculation brings to mind disease transmission—including HIV, hepatitis B and C, and sexually transmitted diseases (STDs). Being such a dangerous vector of infection, semen has become increasingly seen as grotesque—something feared and unwanted. Unprotected seminal ejaculation during vaginal or anal sex is not the only dangerous practice; semen ejaculated into the mouth, eyes, and nose can transmit herpes, chlamydia, syphilis, and gonorrhea.

As a result of these risks, exposure to semen is evermore regulated within the sex entertainment industry. California's Division of Occupational Safety and Health (CAL-OSHA) oversees and regulates workers in the adult film industry; most porn films are produced in southern California. The agency provides adult film workers with safety guidelines and employment protection from work practices that might expose them to blood and "other potentially infectious material (OPIM)."[11] According to CAL-OSHA's website, "semen and vaginal fluid are always considered OPIM." The website also provides examples of "engineering and work practice controls" used in the adult film industry.

In September 2004, CAL-OSHA issued the first ever violations for health and safety regulations to Evasive Angles and T.T. Boy Productions.[12] These violations were for allegedly allowing actors to perform unprotected sex and were specifically related to HIV exposure. During April and May 2004, five adult film actors tested HIV-positive. Subsequent investigation determined that four of the cases were found to be linked. After detecting the transmissions, more than 50 performers who were thought to have had unprotected sex with one of the HIV-positive actors or one of their onscreen partners agreed to a voluntary work quarantine. Following this lead, 12 companies then agreed to a production moratorium until HIV testing of the actors was completed. Production then resumed, presumably with stricter adherence to OSHA guidelines.

In the sex entertainment industry, some film studios demand regular HIV tests. Adult Industry Medical Health Care Foundation (AIM), a nonprofit health-care foundation concerned with sex worker mental and physical health, provides on-site testing services for performers and encourages the responsible sharing of test results between working partners. Yet there have been HIV transmission cases within the pornography industry. As reporter Ann Regentin explains:

> In 1986, John Holmes contracted the virus and continued to work without telling anyone until 1988, when he died of AIDS. In 1998, a rash of HIV cases seemed to point to Marc Wallice, who tested positive for the virus and had been caught working with faked HIV test results. In 1999, Tony Montana tested positive and immediately stopped working. As far as anyone knows, he did not infect anyone else.[13]

Recently, on April 12, 2004, porn star Darren James, who contracted the virus while shooting in Brazil, infected others through work, leading to a brief shutdown of production within the San Fernando Valley. Clearly, there are occupational risks to working in the porn industry, but these can be mitigated through precautions and regulations. Within the sex entertainment industry, then, this bodily fluid straddles the line between being supremely erotic and a lethal weapon.

Each sex worker must develop methods, practices, and professional expertise to avoid exposure to potential diseases or lethal toxins. Furthermore, fertile female sex workers must also try to limit their risk of pregnancy, an occupational hazard of frequent contact with semen. As one of my informants related to me, sex work includes aspects of "hazardous waste material" management. There are different risks associated with exposure to semen by sex workers in the porn industry. Reviewing a working partner's HIV tests is one industry standard. With the advantage of not performing sex in real time, actors and actresses in the porn industry are able to manipulate some exposure to seminal ejaculation. For example, a porn star can appear to swallow ejaculate without actually doing so. During an interview, Raylene, a porn star, stated, "I don't swallow that often because I really don't like the taste. I mean I have, but I don't really like it."[14]

Because I am a feminist scholar, it's important for me to discuss some of the effects of pornography. Pornography and sex work are systems of immense complexity. Some view these enterprises as inherently

oppressive to women because they reinforce existing gender stereotypes about male domination. While, indeed, an overwhelming number of representations of the dominance and subordination of women
by men exist, porn and sex work can also pervert and push conventional ideas about sex and gender roles. For example, in pornography
women can dominate men and be shown to be in control of the sex act—
in fact, dominatrix films could be considered a genre unto itself. Thus,
both women and men can fully and unapologetically desire being dominated. Through offering such niches, pornography creates representations based on sexual fantasy that are often outside the bounds of current sexual mores. In so doing, sexual expression and entertainment
have the potential to warp certain power relationships and entrenched
systems of domination. However, while subversive renderings and
readings of pornography certainly exist, they do not seem to flourish in
the fairly standard and derivative heterosexual, male-dominated, and
frankly predictable sex entertainment industry that now exists.

THE MONEY SHOT

Some recent mainstream films use semen in a different way: as props
for gags or as symbols of alienation. The actual appearance of sperm in
mainstream films is a relatively new phenomenon and perhaps can be
seen, in some ways, as an extension of the increasingly graphic and "re-
alistic" images of the body that are so commonplace today, especially in
television crime and medical dramas. Here severed limbs, burnt bodies,
and gaping wounds are regularly featured, but we often even "go inside" the body to see the actual source of the disease, parasite, or infected organ.

Given the intensely graphic nature of such shows, and given that
sperm has long been readily seen and featured in pornographic films, it
is perhaps not surprising that the once-taboo substance now makes its
appearance in mainstream movies. In the film *Magnolia*, for example,
protagonist Frank Mackey (played by Tom Cruise), is a motivational
speaker for a seminar series, "Seduce and Destroy," which includes a
session entitled "How to turn your 'friend' into your sperm receptacle,"
encouraging insecure men to use their sperm as a means of conquering
and depositing waste into the female body. Taking this a step further,
films like *There's Something About Mary* and *The Squid and the Whale* use

sperm as, in the former, hair gel and, in the latter, a means for acting out adolescent angst. Such material would once have been considered obscene but is now enough of a novelty in mainstream film that it is capable of grabbing the audience's attention and eliciting somewhat shocked laughs.

Film theorist Greg Tuck has suggested that "ejaculation does not merely reference phallic pleasure—it seems it is phallic pleasure."[15] In his analysis of *There's Something About Mary*, he notes that Mary's use of Ted's ejaculate as hair gel can be understood in two seemingly disparate ways. On the one hand, because the seminal ejaculate is both degrading to female bodies because of the stigmatizing act of being "jizzed" upon, the placement of the semen on Mary's body is a misogynistic act that pollutes her and casts her as a fool. On the other hand, the belief that women love seminal ejaculation fulfills a male fantasy of acceptance, and so Mary's acceptance of Ted's fluid may "represent a more utopian fantasy" whereby the "power of abjection" that seminal ejaculation elicits is overcome by love and attraction.

Such treatment of semen is a far cry from its standard depiction in pornographic films. Far from providing comedic relief, semen, as much as the actors often has a starring and very important role to play in these features—as already noted, the man's ejaculation is the raison d'être for these films. The money shot, where a man ejaculates on screen, is the compulsory display of semen in most pornographic films and a number of pornographic magazines as well. Ejaculation, the release of seminal fluid often with astounding force, authenticates the pornographic film in that the sexual desire, the arousal, and the performance are seemingly based on "real" desire. As a male friend quipped to me during a more explosive money shot, "Now you can't fake that." The cum shot is typically defined where a man ejaculates onto a woman, usually onto her face (referred to as a facial) or sometimes onto her sex organs. To be classified as a money shot, the semen must be clearly visible. The "money" refers to the money the actor receives as payout for making the film, which sometimes includes a bonus for the act of ejaculation.

As rhetoric professor Linda Williams discusses in her book, *Hard Core*, "Probably the most striking way that the feature-length hard-core film signals the narrative conclusion of sexual action, however, is through the new convention of external penile ejaculation—or, to use the jargon of the industry, the 'the money shot.'"[16] According to Cindy Patton, money shots "enhance the illusion of control over ejaculation" and further establish the cultural significance and normalcy of orgasm as male and ejaculatory.[17]

When seminal ejaculation is the denouement of a film, there is a presumption about those watching the film. As Patton states, "Even though not everyone in this culture has a penis, the cinematic conventions which position the viewer as the person coming are fairly seamless, and it is quite easy to imagine that this is your penis, regardless of your anatomical configuration."[18] In the porn film, we are each beckoned to identify with that penis and to experience the rush of relief as ejaculate spews forth. Furthermore, Patton has argued that after the wild abandon of pornographic sex, seminal ejaculation enables the man to be responsible for the restoration of sexual order.[19] The stylized repetition of money shots is alluring in that it signals release of control, pleasure, achievement, and success.

It is not clear at what historical moment the money shot emerged as a cinematic convention, but Patton suggests that it has at least existed in the United States since the 1930s as "handmade gay male pornographic drawings from the interwar years."[20] The male orgasm demonstrated through ejaculation indicates the completion of a sex act, the scene, the movie, the book, and the encounter. It instructs the audience that the activity is over and has been successful. As an industry standard of pornographic films, the money shot was fairly commonplace after World War II.[21] Pornography became a growth industry and was soon responsible for driving many economic markets. In the late 1970s, as historians John D'Emilio and Estelle Freedman point out, "soon, the rental of pornographic movies was providing the essential margin of profit for many video stores."[22] Frederick Lane, author of *Obscene Profits: The Entrepreneurs of Pornography in the Cyber Age,* claims that, "without question, pornography has been the World Wide Web's major economic success."[23]

Who is watching this pornography? Men, overwhelmingly. In some ways, pornography replicates existing ways that boys and men are presumed to view the world, and especially visual entertainment. For many boys, watching and consuming sports is a rite of passage and proof of their burgeoning heterosexual masculinity. Sporting events focus on acts of superiority and inferiority, rituals of humiliation, and feats of domination and submission. If we think of the sports slow motion replay, we realize that men have been visually instructed to understand and expect the use of slow motion and multiple replays of physical interaction from various angles through their lifelong spectatorship of sports. As journalist Pamela Paul found in her face-to-face interviews of over 80 men about their porn-watching habits, most men masturbate when they watch porn.[24] Furthermore, using multiple studies of men's pornography habits, Paul posits that adolescent male pressures of measuring up to high standards of masculinity are apt to be seduced by porn:

> The rejected male, particularly during his teenage years when he is most apt to discover porn, is constantly subjected to humiliation and frustration. Each rejection gets tucked away into the private place where men mull over their excessive body hair, and insufficient pay-checks; where pride is swallowed and humbleness dwells, accumulating the emotional debris of ongoing denial and frustrated desire. And this becomes the emotional impetus that brings them to pornography and the ineffable release of masturbation.[25]

Fred Fejes, a professor of communications, has written that "heterosexual male identity is grounded in an overarching gender based heterosexual regime of power and domination,"[26] but many other scholars, including Patton and Williams, have made the point that, in porn, men are watching other men ejaculate. Much of the porn scene is about the achievement and impressive display of ejaculation—the force of ejaculate, the amount, the direction, the aim, and the control. Aren't men impressed with other men's performances? Aren't these physical acts impressive to other men, just as are other feats of physical prowess like hitting a home run or running a touchdown? Perhaps this explains the recent London *Times* headline, "Pornography Increases the Quality of Men's Sperm," which featured a story based on evolutionary biologists' research on the effects of viewing pornography on sperm quality.[27] Using the theory of sperm competition, the story explains how men who view heterosexual pornography increased their production of fertile sperm. In this way, the very act of viewing pornography can strike at the nerve of male competitiveness and make said males more fertile.

Yet viewing pornography can be a heterosexual training ground and a means to experience male bonding, as often the films are watched by groups of men. Such acts clearly give rise to homoeroticism, or the experience of being sexually aroused by one's own sex. This spectatorship has historically been experienced by groups of men at stag parties, frat houses, movie theaters, and backroom bars.[28] But now men are watching other men alone at home on DVD, video, digital cable, and the internet. As Patton has argued, porn has been domesticated and now takes place in the privacy of one's own home, perhaps after attending to all the chores of mundane everyday life. So the assumed spectatorship—and thus the driving force behind the industry—are men (and secondarily women) watching other men ejaculate: on sheets, women's faces, women's backs, in cups, in the air. Women's orgasms, while they may be portrayed, are not depicted in any clear visual fashion. And while there is a niche market for female ejaculation films, it is still predominantly an all-male "money shot" genre.

GIRLS GONE WILD FOR SPERM

There is a new niche market of seminal ejaculate films that expand on the glorification of men's ejaculate. Unlike other pornographic genres, these movies focus on semen as the central theme of the narrative and the action, not solely the denouement. Titles such as *Semen Demons, Desperately Seeking Semen, The Cum Cocktail, We Swallow, Sperm Overdose* (volumes 1–6), *Sperm Dreams, Sperm Burpers* (volumes 1–5), *A Splash of Sperm*, and *Feeding Frenzy* (volumes 1–3) venture beyond the money shot toward eroticizing seminal ingestion. The contents of the promotional descriptions of the videos, as well as the videos themselves, depict a variety of women drinking and bathing in semen from diverse male partners. Women appear to be insatiable and competitive about their desire for ingesting the semen as they rush to get to the ejaculating penis, the full shot glass, or residual ejaculate on a sheet. What does it mean to see women completely overcome with their desire to drink semen? To smear it all over their bodies? What does this say about male desire and masculinity? Here is a sampling of promotional descriptions of a few films:[29]

Promo for the movie *Semen Shots 2*

> There's nothing that a pretty girl likes more at the end of a sexual encounter than to drink her lover's cum out of a shot glass. That's the premise behind this developing series, anyway. Delilah Strong entertains five young men and takes two cocks in her pussy before

swigging multiple shots of their hot spunk. Jasmyn Taliana whimpers a lot before downing her two shots. Mason Storm enjoys a bit of anal before laughing her way through two fingers of warm sperm. Rio Mariah takes a double penetration and then squeezes the contents of her pussy and ass into a glass for savoring. Monica Sweetheart looks pretty in a sheer nightie with sparkly flowers during her anal and still looks cute while tossing back some of Brian Pumper's love cocktail.

Promo for *Crème de la Face 22*

The man who seems to manufacture Elmer's Glue with his gonads is back and doing his thing with another crop of Seattle girls. This time out, things get rolling as Mr. Rodney Moore and Red get sloppy blowjobs from Kayla, a big-tittied black girl who knows well the value of slobber and its application in oral lovemaking. The twin shots of creamy white nut nougat she catches at the climax of her labors stand in vivid contrast to her smooth brown skin. Later on, Twilite Moon approaches Moore on the street and asks him to come home with her so she can shoot a porno. Moon has hairy underarms and a delta that's grown into a jungle. The Rodster bones her butt, deposits a load in her mouth and then, once she's spit the gob out into a glass, uses it to glaze her armpit fur.

Promo for *Wad Gobblers, Volume 13*

This video begins with an amazing wild montage of twelve or fourteen chicks all taking it in the face with gobs of splashing semen, a dozen or more beauties being blasted with emissions so powerful it shoots up their nostrils. Their tongues snake out to lap up every drop and the overflow bubbles like lava out of their mouths.

These descriptions of money shots use sensational linguistic cues to entice the reader to purchase or rent these videos. It is obvious that seminal ejaculation is the main attraction in each video, the star of the show. Women's bodies are the surfaces for seminal display or the containers to ingest semen. Using the props of shot glasses and cocktail accessories, women literally become drunk on semen, often losing control in the presence of such powerful and intoxicating fluids.

Ironically, this genre of pornography is being produced against a cultural backdrop in which semen is directly associated with risk. Warnings about HIV/AIDS and STDs are plastered on bus stops, broadcast through public service announcements on radio and television, and echoed in health-care interactions. We are told to avoid semen to lessen our risk of pregnancy, disease, and death. Some industries, such as health care and forensics, have worked to imbue the raw material of semen with risk. Similarly, fertility enterprises and spouse or partner surveillance companies market their services by both reminding us of the risk of seminal ejaculate and claiming to mitigate that risk for us.

But the constant messages about risk and danger from seminal ejaculate have likely affected men's own relationship to their semen, as well as amplified a sense of it as forbidden. These pornographic videos then capitalize on recovering and eroticizing the raw material of semen as safe, natural, organic, whole. The commodification of semen in these videos relies on a specific form of consumption in the narrative arc. Taking the action a moment beyond the money shot, the triumph of these videos is actually the expression of reverence for semen as it is placed either in a shot glass or on a woman's face, buttocks, or breasts. The absence of, or disregard for, risk is also a saleable dimension of these videos. They sell the image of sperm as not embodying risk or, even if risky, then certainly worth that risk. In these films, these female actors are depicted as willing to debase themselves, put themselves at risk, and even become sick in order to please their men. (A fate that is a real hazard of the job, as already mentioned.)

There seems to be general consensus, if only from anecdotal evidence, that the taste of semen is not as delicious as the videos portray. Some have compared the scent of semen to bleach, household cleanser, or swimming pool water. The taste has been described as salty and bitter, which may explain why Semenex, a patented, all-natural powder drink has been created to sweeten semen. Semenex, with an advertised price of $54.95 for a 30-serving container, relies on testimonials similar to this one: "Tasty! I've never really had a problem with semen, except when it gets really bitter, but this product really makes drinking a man down a treat!" so says, Jenni from Mesa, Arizona. As an online ad in *Maxim* magazine claims, "Semenex is where to go for delicious sperm guaranteed. Finally, an answer to the 'I don't like the taste' argument."[30] Interviewed as part of the 2005 documentary *Inside Deep Throat* about the infamous porn movie, Helen Gurley Brown, *Cosmopolitan* editor in chief and author of the 1962 best seller *Sex and the Single Girl,* extols the benefits of semen, saying, "Women have known for years that ejaculate is good for the skin because it is full of babies . . . it's full of protein. Just rub it all over your face, and skin and chest."

While semen may get mixed reviews from actual women, in the world of pornographic films semen is no longer something that is gross, yucky, smells bad, or brings disease—rather, it is something delicious, desired, and needed. Perhaps only the bold fantasy of a world dominated by men, and their need for sexual pleasure, could provide the scenario where women actually fight with each other for the pleasure of guzzling down ounces of semen. As radical feminist and noted critic of pornography Andrea Dworkin stated at a conference at the University of Chicago, "It is a convention of pornography that the sperm is on her, not in her. It marks the spot, what he owns and how he owns it. The ejaculation on her is a way of saying (through showing) that she is contaminated with his dirt; that she is dirty."[31] Yet Dworkin's explanation does not take into account that these actresses exhibit pleasure and that it is their pleasure that many of their male partners enjoy. It is perhaps more accurate to theorize that men, both as spectators and actors, want women to want their semen.

Within the sex industries of prostitution and pornography, sperm maintains contradictory meanings. It is referred to as a dangerous, if not lethal, weapon and, alternatively, as the crowning achievement of human interaction. For sex workers who perform sex acts with actual people (as opposed to pornography film actors), seminal ejaculation is a hazardous waste material to be managed and avoided for fear of pregnancy or disease. Sex workers do not have the benefit of reviewing their partners' HIV test results before a scene. Nor are there multiple takes to "get it right." And since many male clients are socialized by pornographic videos that do not depict safe sex, many sex workers find that, while they must use latex devices to protect themselves, at the same time they must eroticize their safe sex practices or risk failing to perform the job they are being paid for.

"DEALING WITH THE JIZZ": STORIES FROM SEX WORKERS

Most sex workers handle men as if they are dangerous; they can be violent, deceiving, and vectors of disease. Despite this belief about men, most sex workers will take on the risk of intimate physical contact as long as the men have the money to pay for it. This, of course, assumes that men can afford an average $200 an hour sexual experience. In an ironic twist, sex workers and sperm banks have an inverse relationship with regard to sperm and money. Men pay sex workers for their services, which includes managing their potentially dangerous semen, while people pay sperm banks to store or purchase certifiably healthy semen. Semen banks pay donors between $40 and $60 per ejaculate. Each ejaculate can be divided up into between two and three vials, which cost roughly $150 each. So one ejaculate divided into two samples is (150 x 2) – 60 = $240 profit per ejaculate. This is $40 more than the typical sex worker makes.

The analysis that follows is based on interviews conducted over a five-year period (1991–1996) with well-paid, in-call, consenting sex workers. Sex workers occasionally reject clients who use heavy drugs or alcohol, are on the bad trick list, or simply give them the creeps. A bad trick list circulates within communities of sex workers and has the names and descriptions of previously delinquent or violent male clients. Perhaps through personal stigma and immersion in an AIDS/HIV culture, sex workers view all bodily products as having degrees of toxicity. In the pursuit of self-preservation and profit, semen is treated as a carrier of pathogens, germs, and sperm that may debilitate, kill, or impregnate the worker. All sex workers interviewed about their safer sex practices stated they always use a condom for each act of vaginal and anal intercourse. Here are some of their comments about men and their sperm:

> I personally do not want to have any contact with fluids that come out of a man's dick. So like today I saw somebody who had a little pre-ejaculate on his belly and what I do is I take a piece of tissue and I wipe it off, then I take another piece of tissue and I apply nonoxynol nine. (Bonny, 54; 20-year professional dominant)

After a few times with a few guys, you learn to treat them all the same. I mean they can fool you with things and you can think they are actually nice and safe. But basically, I think they are all probably lying. (Olivia, 33; 2-year veteran prostitute)

My party line is rubbers for fucking and rubbers for sucking. I have always been strict about it. (Hadley, 55; 25-year veteran stripper, prostitute, professional dominant)

Because my cleanliness standards are so strict I know it gets on some people's nerves. Cleaning up this pre-ejaculate, it takes a certain amount of planning and time and carefulness to make sure that you are practicing all this safe sex when you're working with somebody who doesn't—who wants to think they're having a spontaneous romantic moment. And it's not like you've got a partner who's thoroughly educated. You sit down and have a discussion beforehand and now you're going to have spontaneous safe sex. You're dealing with somebody who doesn't know shit and you're trying to educate them and have a spontaneous moment with them at the same time. It's hard work. And sometimes I can tell that I'm not getting the cooperation I want and I'm getting a little bit uptight, and they're starting to feel like—one of my clients calls it the "hazardous waste material."
To me I don't want to come in contact with sperm at all. And sometimes when I'm cleaning it off with a piece of tissue a little moisture—I can feel a little moisture on my hands, I immediately go and wash, you know, look careful to try avoid any areas that I have cuts or hangnails. (Michelle, 38; 6-year veteran prostitute)

Men and their semen are viewed here as universally dangerous, distrustful, and dirty. Semen is something that must be managed. No matter how it is represented, as good or bad, or somewhere in between, at the time of its ejaculation, semen has to be dealt with. As Quincy, a 45-year-old sex worker who has been in the industry since her late 20s states,

The guys want me to really like their cum. I think many of them would like to see me roll around in it and drink it and basically bathe in it. Maybe like they see on the movies they watch. But, I can't really do that. So I just sort of pretend. There would be something nice about being able to wallow in body fluids but I am not even going to go there.

As discussed, this desire to "wallow in body fluids" is promoted in almost all pornographic videos, but it is only risk free for the jizzee, not the jizzed upon. Quincy empathizes with her clients about semen, telling them, "I really love sperm and I wish I could swallow it. But we can pretend and I bet you will not even notice the difference." In her sex work career and as a practitioner of latex devices, Quincy claims that men do not know the difference between safer sex and unprotected sex when things are done by a professional. She claims when safer sex is seamlessly accomplished, her male clientele (and perhaps men in general) accept its use: "So it's like a Pavlovian trick to get people more comfortable with and more turned on to the possibility of safe sex. The snap of the glove or smell of condoms means something fun is going to happen."

Sex workers create safety standards for dealing with semen. They use male and female condoms, gloves, and finger cots (small latex coverings for individual fingers), as actual physical barriers that inhibit the semen from making contact with unexposed body surfaces. Safer sex, as a collection of symbols, practices, and technological innovations, both protects sex workers from contamination and assures the client of standard operating procedures that reduce their own exposure to the "hazardous waste material" of previous clients. As Michelle, a 38-year-old petite blonde, states, "When my clients get a little strange about my safer sex stuff, I will say, 'Well, this might bug you a little bit, but I promise to keep you safe' and then I will smile all sweet."

In addition to manipulations for safety purposes, sex workers have crafted techniques to make semen perform more predictably, to make this recalcitrant substance more workable. Sex workers train their clients in techniques for semen control and manipulation. For example, many sex workers instruct their clients on how to put on a condom. They can instruct men in how to maintain erections and delay ejaculation through practicing sex acts and talking about their bodies. By bringing an erect man close to orgasm and then delaying the ejaculation, sex workers talk about building a man's endurance and self-control during sex acts. They work with their clients, talking to them and coaxing them to understand their own bodies and sexual responses. Several of the women I interviewed have developed symbolic rituals of performance to promote pleasurable semen control. They place a variety of male condoms in special places on a night table or at an altar with candles and incense, "To honor the act they know will be coming soon," as Olivia put it. Most sex workers opened up male condoms during our interviews to demonstrate different techniques for placing condoms on imaginary penises using their mouth and hands, coaching men through the safer sex requirements with statements like, "Now comes the fun part," and, "I can't wait. Can you?"

When I was interviewing Michelle at her apartment, she invited me to look at an album of erotic photographs of herself in full makeup and dressed in lingerie. "This is how I look when my clients come over," she explained as we explored the ironies of attempting to be sexy and available while assiduously managing men's ejaculate. Michelle knows that in her work she cannot use the universal precautions of the health-care industry to protect herself. Rather, she must maintain her sexy, available, and pleasurable image while ensuring her survival:

> I mean going to see my dentist becomes—I feel like a hazardous waste material myself. First he had some new goggles, well then he got a shield, you know, and next I expect him to come in just like—you know, a space suit next time. It's so funny. But that's what we're having to do. See the medical profession has the luxury of looking like they're in this space suit. I can't look like I'm in a space suit. I have got to look like I'm being very intimate and everything, and yet really I am trying to have my own little space suit going on here.

Ana, a 38-year-old petite, brunette sex worker, explained one of the ways she flatters men while retrieving used condoms:

> It's funny because I started doing this thing with the condoms. When I take them off the guy, before I throw them away or flush them down the toilet, I show them to the guy. . . . I mean most guys because a couple of my guys might be out the door before I get a chance. But when I show them to the guy, I say something like, "Wow you must really like me a lot" or "I have never seen this much before." Lots of guys seem to really like that when you tell them that they have a lot [of semen]. They kind of get off on it.

This verbal acknowledgement and visual display of seminal volume echoes the penis size concerns explored at the beginning of this chapter.

Ana is exploiting a man's concern with size, density, and volume as a way to praise men and continue the pleasurable (safer) sexual experience. If seminal ejaculate were not contained in a condom, how else might a man know how virile he apparently is?

In spite of the acknowledged risks, sex workers are handling semen and managing men. In many instances, sex workers innovate containment strategies to limit exposure to semen while also making men feel good about their semen and their expressions of masculinity. Through the use of flattery, men are encouraged to believe they measure up or exceed other men's performances and bodies. Sex workers' (like Ana's) use of male condoms enables them to capture semen. In this context, semen is used to compliment a man on his potency. By empathizing with men about the "good old days," sex workers can enforce rules about seminal exposure, while making men feel that their semen is not hazardous. Sex workers' expertise at using latex devices enables them to make men feel taken care of, while assuring their own safety from exposure.

THE ESSENCE OF (EVERY)MAN

With the proliferation of movies and videos that glorify the money shot, the sex entertainment industry provides an avenue for men to be spectators in the celebration of unprocessed, carnal, natural semen. Unlike other industries that manage semen, such as scientific laboratories, fertility clinics, and forensics enterprises, male bodily products do not need to be technologically enhanced or scientifically manipulated to be useful or understood. Unlike the workers in these industries, porn stars do not use universal precautions of covering their bodies with latex gloves, goggles, and face masks when handling semen. In real life, most sex workers, particularly the successful ones, are not entirely cloaked in thin layers of plastic, rigidly carrying out state-regulated mandates for handling body fluids. Sex workers, in films and real life, are either very minimally dressed or naked and do not shrink away from intimate contact with seminal fluid.

As other industries that manage sperm have established, not all men are created equal. For example, a majority of men who attempt to donate sperm are rejected from sperm banks. And even outside of the fertility clinics, there are multiple reminders that most men produce semen that is gross, diseased, genetically inferior, incompetent, lazy, and unwanted. To some extent, then, the pornography industry produces images that address the needs and desires of these men. That is, since men are socialized to believe that their semen is undesirable and even disgusting to women, and possibly perceived as a health hazard, it is a relief to see representations of their semen as cherished. The raw material of male desire, seminal fluid, is produced directly from the source, and it is wanted and desperately desired in its purest form.

In these videos, there is still power associated with the man's characteristics, but power and social desirability is also assigned to the color, amount, and image of the semen itself—and the woman's positive reaction to it. No one is running to the bathroom to spit out the ejaculate, and everyone swallows with a smile. Semen, in these videos, is not abstracted into a characterization—it is not anthropomorphized—yet it is still desirable. Furthermore, the fairly recently established niche genres that focus on the consumption of semen depict women who can't get enough. They have no fear and no disgust for the substance in its natural state. No technological manipulation of semen is necessary.

While this process of appreciating everyman's sperm may seem liberating, it is still occurring within systems of male domination. The forces of hegemonic masculinity act to subjugate some men to the control of other men deemed more worthy, esteemed, or powerful. These fantasies about seminal consumption sell subjugated men the belief that they are the epitome of traditionally masculine power when they may rank quite low. While some men may opt out of a traditionally masculine set of behaviors and work to redefine masculinity, other men will literally buy in to the images and tropes of pornography. Those men who are still participating in and consenting to a process that devalues them become perfect consumers of films that bolster the story of male dominance. This means that, even though these men may not directly benefit from hierarchal relations of masculine power, they will support films that depict male domination because they identify with the male protagonist. Porn becomes one of the many opiates of the wimpy men who cannot take a stand against the ultimate nonconsensual subordination of others because they themselves are so subordinated. In this way, hegemonic masculinity maintains its dominance by providing commodities that work to placate those oppressed by activities that are in reality disempowering.

My analysis of semen as represented, consumed, and manipulated within industrial and commercial sex markets further establishes sperm's elasticity of meaning. While individual men may be aware of their social worth as subordinate to other men, commercial sex work is one arena in which men can retain hope that their seminal ejaculate, their essence of manhood, is enjoyed, powerful, and spectacular.

5

The Family Jewels

Sperm Banks and the Crisis of Fatherhood

On March 20, the first day of spring, I spent a long day visiting New York City's American Museum of Natural History with my daughters, Georgia and Grace. We went to the Cosmic Collisions exhibit at the Hayden Planetarium and then walked through Central Park, scampering up huge rocks and naming flowers along the way. It was one of those days that my older daughter describes as "everything clicking." When I returned to Brooklyn, I prepared to teach an evening class. The phone rang, and it was a call from TSBC, the Sperm Bank of California. Karla was calling to check in with me about our donor. At first I thought it was a telemarketing fundraiser and automatically responded, "Sorry, I'm not interested. Please take me off the list." But Karla continued, "We are calling people to see if they would like to purchase any of the inventory of previous donors. These are donors whose inventory we are going to be destroying. We had held some aside for siblings, and we were wondering if you might like to store some vials?"

I was speechless for an awkward moment. "I don't understand—you are going to destroy his sperm?" The donor's profile jumped to mind, and I tried to imagine how he might feel knowing this.

Karla patiently replied, "Yes, we had held it aside for siblings and since we haven't had requests for some time, we are going to be destroying it. But we are checking in with any families who have had pregnancies in order to see if anyone would want any siblings." I repressed an urge to ask how many families she was calling for this particular donor, perhaps other families were scooping up the vials, a run on the spermatic market, I thought. Instead, I asked, "How many vials are left?"

"There are eight IUI vials and about four of the unwashed." I started to think out loud: "I feel like I should buy it because I just don't want it to be destroyed. I mean that just seems too final. But I don't think I will have any more children. But then again maybe I should just keep it on ice in case I change my mind." I thought about how much it might cost to store semen I didn't even know if I would use. I continued, "I don't know if I should say no for now. And I also think I should probably speak to my partner about it."

"That is fine, you have a couple of weeks to decide and then we will destroy it. If you should call back, ask for Karla."

I was jarred by the phone call. On the one hand, I was convinced that I should purchase the entire inventory. I wanted to keep the possibility of more children alive, even if my partner has been abundantly clear about not wanting more children. On the other hand, as I thought about it, I suddenly realized that I could still have more children without that particular donor's sperm. My mind then jumped to other scenarios: What if Georgia got some strange disease, and I needed to have a sibling for some form of organ donation or transfusion? I rationalized that if need be, we could always make some desperate plea to contact the donor.

As I prepared to leave for work, I felt pangs of guilt as I kissed Georgia goodbye. Am I letting part of her be destroyed? After a discussion with my girlfriend, I felt more confident in our decision to "let go" of the remaining vials. The experience was a reminder of the ways in which using a sperm bank reverberates in our lives in unexpected ways.

There are roughly 4 million children born annually in the United States. The U.S. sperm banking industry estimates that 30,000 of these children are conceived through donor sperm. Who are all these children, and how do they make sense of having a donor for a daddy? From October 2005 through March 2006, the *New York Times* ran a series of articles about sperm donation (figure 5.1).[1]

One such article, "Hello, I'm Your Sister: Our Father Is Donor 150," explores the recently created website donorsiblingregistry.com. In operation for three years, this fee-for-information site enables parents, donors, offspring, and siblings to locate one another through sperm donor identification numbers. This *New York Times* front-page story was the most emailed item for two days in a row, clearly suggesting the interest in the topic to a wide range of people. The registry, which has led to over 1,000 matches, enables half-siblings to connect with each other.

Many half-siblings report that this connection is a positive experience. As the journalist Amy Harmon states:

Figure 5.1. Cover of *New York Times Magazine* featuring one in a series of articles about semen banks and availability of male partners. From Jennifer Egan, "Wanted: A Few Good Sperm," *New York Times Magazine,* March 19, 2006.

While many donor-conceived children prefer to call their genetic father "donor," to differentiate the biological function of fatherhood from the social one, they often feel no need to distance themselves, linguistically or emotionally, from their siblings. Justin, 15, of Denver, was the most recent half-sibling to surface in a group that now numbers five. After his newfound family attended his recent choir concert, Justin's mother, Susy Senk, overheard him introducing them to his friends with a self-styled sing-song, "This is my sister from another mother, and this is my brother from another mother, this is my other sister from another mother" and so on.[2]

It seems that while the newly discovered half-sibling is integrated into a family tree with relative ease, the notion of a sperm donor being a father is not as clear-cut. While fathers and sperm donors clearly have very different roles, responsibilities, and expectations regarding their relationships with their offspring, the notion of paternity, although not a clear-cut indicator, is still linked to fatherhood.

A primary reason that donors are not thought of as fathers is related to the U.S. sperm banking industry preference for donor anonymity. But the market for donated sperm is changing. In another article, "Are You My Sperm Donor? Few Clinics Will Say," Harmon claims that anonymity generates fear among semen recipients. The potential for misrepresentation of the donors, uncontrolled use of donors for multiple births, and the lack of access to health information of donors as they age may be exacerbated by a culture of anonymity. Some European countries, such as Switzerland and the Netherlands, have recently instituted policies to ban anonymous donation of gametes.[3] Citing the right of a child to know his or her biological identity, the Swiss law guarantees the child "access to data concerning his lineage." But Harmon points out that these regulations have "resulted in a steep decline in donors, which has made sperm banks and fertility clinics [in the United States] more determined to oppose mandatory identity disclosure."[4]

The drop in donations due to mandatory identity disclosure in Europe suggests that many donors may be reluctant to donate, due to the possibility of their sperm being traced back to them. In my experience at TSBC, the majority of donors preferred to remain anonymous. This preference for anonymity is also reflected in sperm banks' fees; because it is more difficult to procure, identity-release semen is often more expensive than anonymous semen. Additionally, while a few donors have registered on donorsiblingregistry.com, it is mostly mothers and children who are creating the profiles. Could it be the expectations of the social role of fatherhood that frightens donors away from providing identifying information? What are the deeper connections between notions of fatherhood, fathers' rights, sperm donors' rights, and children's rights?

To gain insight into questions such as these, it is necessary to understand how sperm has come to embody the extremes of masculinity—the best and worst notions of what we think it is to be a man. In this chapter, I examine the positive extreme: how sperm represents aspects of the ideal man in the worlds of science, medicine, commerce, and politics. In the preceding chapters, I discuss that, throughout history, our understanding of sperm is directly related to social, cultural, and religious ideas about men and masculinity. But the current context in which these representations are being constructed is unprecedented: as technological advances and social changes have made sperm more accessible to more people than ever before, a virtual land grab has ensued among opposing parties over the meaning, use, and ownership of sperm. In each example presented here, sperm's embodiment of protomasculine attributes is both purposeful and problematic. For some, sperm has become a source of professionalization—seed money, if you will—for enterprises in the fertility industry. Others find that the increasing accessibility of vials of sperm enables reproduction outside of constricting heterosexual relations. And for still others, sperm's perceived misuse has been a lightning rod and source of mobilization for the fatherhood rights movement.

BANKING ON SPERM

Since 1550, when Bartholomeus Eustacus recommended that a husband use his fingers to help semen reach his wife's cervix to improve the chances of conception, much advancement has been made in our understanding of the human body and the role semen plays in reproduction. Beyond mere guidance, and removed from the human body, the technique of freezing and preserving semen with semen extenders (a solution added to an ejaculate to enhance and extend the potency of semen), then injecting it into a female animal, was first developed for use with livestock (cattle, horses, and goats).[5] This practice became widespread from the 1940s through the 1960s. These advances grew into a booming industry among humans that is now known as sperm banking.

The historical emergence of human semen cryopreservation (freezing semen) dates back to Italy in 1776. Lazzaro Spallanzani, an Italian priest, physiologist, and natural scientist, reported freezing human semen in snow and then retrieving motile sperm. He is also credited with performing some of the first successful artificial insemination experiments on animals, including dogs. In the United States, the first documented semen bank began in 1950 at the University of Iowa.[6] These early banks were exclusively part of the university system until the early 1970s. The university provided the materials, funding, and legitimacy to further explore, research, and develop clinical applications, leading to the first work on humans in 1954. In 1972, commercial semen banks were established for infertile men who were presumably married to women and wanted to have children.[7] This new wave of semen banking followed on the heels of the modern birth control movement, which gave the pill to women and the vasectomy to men.

Through the 1980s, the semen banking industry would continue to grow. J. K. Sherman, one of the pioneers in sperm banking, wrote in 1979:

> I predict, however, that there will be a more intense interest in cryobanking for AI (artificial insemination), primarily in pre-therapy storage and in job related pre-exposure storage as protection against both deliberate and accidental exposure to environmental agents which may compromise fertility, or even worse, compromise normal progeny.[8]

As Sherman predicted, many men, especially those vasectomized or undergoing chemotherapy, now use sperm banks as a storage facility— similar to a safety deposit box for precious valuables at a financial bank. This type of "fertility insurance" is marketed by sperm banks (and by the military in times of combat) to alleviate fears of exposure to substances that are considered harmful or lethal to sperm and men. For example, during the first Gulf War, there was a marked increase in semen storage requests as soldiers faced the real threat of losing life and limb or being exposed to toxins that could injure their fertility.[9] Both single men concerned about future reproductive possibilities and married couples wanting to keep reproductive options open to a possibly widowed soldier's wife have used sperm banks.

The growth of the sperm banking industry was also driven by other forces, some of which were neither planned nor predicted. Single women, lesbians, and unmarried heterosexual couples also now use semen banks in order to reproduce. Ultimately, new definitions of reproduction have emerged as the traditional American homemaker's turkey baster has been transformed into a means of independence from traditional heterosexual, monogamous, married families.

As the sperm banking industry and its customer base have grown and diversified, so has the need for industry regulations. The American Association of Tissue Banks (AATB) and the American Fertility Society (AFS) play significant regulatory roles, having developed the standards and conventions of semen regulation. For example, by 1990, in response to the AIDS crisis, sperm banks adopted a six-month cryopreservation standard that requires the donor be tested for HIV twice, first when he made the donation and then six months later (six months being the amount of time HIV antibodies may develop in the blood of the donor). This procedure is now a requirement of the AFS's guidelines. This policy enables the donor to be retested for HIV before releasing the semen for insemination purposes, thus ensuring that the virus will not be passed on.

In addition to private and professional organizations, the federal government is also involved in the regulation of sperm banks and their products. As of January 2003, all facilities that handle human cells and tissue, including eggs and sperm, must register with the Food and Drug Administration (FDA), which also began mandating the testing of donors for diseases such as hepatitis and HIV. But the FDA's regulatory role is relatively recent. Since 1976, the AATB, "a scientific, not-for-profit, peer group organization founded to facilitate the provision of transplantable tissues of uniform high quality in quantities sufficient to meet national needs" has been accrediting sperm banks.[10] The AATB's board of governors is made up of insiders—scientists and executive directors of semen banks—who set guidelines for accreditation. The three-year accreditation process includes an inspection by an AATB physician, as well as a commitment to practice in accordance with AATB standards. Regulation is currently conducted through a loose collaboration between the AATB, the FDA, and the U. S. Department of Health and Human Services (DHHS). Some states have guidelines regarding sperm banks, and when transporting semen across state lines, banks must also adhere to the DHHS guidelines for transportation of human biologics. As of May 2004, the DHHS—through the FDA's Center for Biologics Evaluation and Research (CBER)—mandates testing for several diseases: human immunodeficiency virus (HIV), types 1 and 2; hepatitis B virus

(HBV); hepatitis C virus (HCV); human transmissible spongiform encephalopathy (TSE), Creutzfeldt-Jakob disease (CJD), and *Treponema pallidum* (syphilis); human T-lymphotropic virus (HTLV), types I and II; *Chlamydia trachomatis;* and *Neisseria gonorrhea.*[11]

Sperm banks also play a major part in the donor insemination process. First reported in 1884, donor insemination (DI) is a simple procedure, as described by the Boston Women's Health Book Collective:

> You suck the semen into a needleless hypodermic syringe (some women use an eye dropper or a turkey baster), gently insert the syringe into your vagina while lying flat on your back with your rear up on a pillow, and empty the syringe into your vagina to deposit the semen as close to your cervix as possible.[12]

Although this clear, how-to account succeeds at demystifying the insemination procedure, increasingly complex processes have transformed donor insemination into an elaborate event, requiring the assistance of a variety of medical workers. Indeed, now many groups and individuals are indirectly involved in this procedure, including the AATB and the AFS, physicians and other health-care providers, stockholders, donors, consumers, and their potential offspring.

Today, there are three types of sperm banks: university-affiliated, commercial, and nonprofit. After developing and refining the insemination technologies throughout the 1970s, university sperm banks (affiliated with teaching hospitals) became strictly noncommercial patient banks where semen is frozen and stored for pre-vasectomy, and pre-chemotherapy and radiation treatment patients only. Commercial banks are now the most popular forms of sperm banks in the country. Commercial sperm banks cement a relationship with physicians by requiring that all semen be sent directly to the doctor performing the insemination. In other words, the average person cannot buy and obtain semen without a doctor's okay. An exception to this can be found in the published philosophy of the nonprofit Sperm Bank of California: "We believe that women have the right to control their own reproduction and in doing so, determine if, when and how to achieve pregnancy." Congruent with these progressive values, the Sperm Bank of California is the only nonprofit sperm bank in the United States, excluding those that are affiliated with universities.

RUNNING THE BANK

With stockholders and financial portfolios, commercial semen banks often are large enterprises offering multiple reproductive services; as such, they compete with each other for market share. Perhaps the most important way sperm banks advertise themselves to potential customers is through their donor catalogues. A closer look at such catalogues reveals their efforts to convince the woman or couple that they are choosing a particular man rather than sticky, wriggly, little cells. Sperm may be disembodied, but they are vividly personified as pliable, healthy, agile, fertile, and socially desirable.

Sperm banks most often begin by highlighting their procedures. Screening procedures are detailed as a way to ensure trust in the integrity of the sample—for example: "Only 4% of men who inquire [as donors] are selected," or "We usually eliminate 90% of all candidates." Such percentages attest to the intense selectivity of the men invited to participate in this enterprise. Furthermore, donor catalogue listings of possible donor semen invites the customer to compare the prescreened (successful) donors, so they can pick the best semen for the job. The donor narratives read like personal ads, capturing the recipients' imaginations as they search for the ideal—ethnicity, height, weight, eyes, hair, build, complexion, blood type, interests, and activities:

> This profile is for Erik who is a Caucasian/Scandinavian. He is 5–11 tall and weighs 167 lbs. He has Brown eyes and Dark Brown hair. He is a B.S. Student and his blood type is A–. He likes hiking and has a black belt in karate.[13]

The ad-like narratives serve as a powerful teaser to entice recipients to invest in the longer donor profiles, usually made available for an additional fee.

Sperm banks automatically test donors and their semen samples for a variety of sexually transmitted diseases. For an additional price, genetic testing is also available at the recipient's request. Also available beyond the many tests for STDs and genetic defects, semen can be centrifuged in the "swim up" method, designed for pre-sex selection[14] and analyzed for motility to provide evidence of speed. Just over the horizon, there are new technologies currently being reviewed by the FDA. For example, flow cytometry, or the measurement of cells and color dyeing of cells as they flow by a detector, can be conducted on a semen sample to determine if a sperm cell is X or Y bearing, and then the sperm of preference can be used for insemination. Flow cytometry has a success rate of 60 to 70 percent for conceiving a child of the desired sex and was expected to be made available to consumers in 2007. The growth of this practice has the potential to radically transform the ways in which individuals consider family planning, birth order, and family composition.

Another metric offered for "semen quality" is its statistical success rate as determined by the number of successful pregnancies from the bank. The quantity and range of fees and services sometimes resembles a Chinese take-out menu. Prices vary, depending on which bank you choose.[15] For example, the nonprofit Sperm Bank of California's (TSBC) fees for these tests and procedures are typically lower than those at the for-profit California Cryobank (CC): a vial of anonymous donor sperm for regular, unwashed intracervical insemination (ICI) at home is $255 at TSBC and $315 at CC. Washed and IUI-ready (semen is washed to prepare it for intrauterine insemination by a health practitioner) anonymous donor sperm is $295 per vial at TSBC compared with $380 at CC. Then there is the more expensive identity-release sperm, provided through a program that enables a child to receive contact information from a donor at age 18. ICI identity-release donor sperm is $330 (TSBC) to $415 (CC), and washed IUI-ready identity-release donor sperm is $380 (TSBC) to $480 (CC) per vial. These fees do not include tank rental or shipping and handling, which range between $100 and $175. The additional donor information fees are more comparable between banks. The donor medical chart (15–20 pages, including family health history) is $15. The practice of donor photo matching where a photo of a recipient or their partner is matched to a donor's photo is $50. Men storing semen for their spouse or intimate partner must pay $250 for an initial semen storage visit or consultation, plus a nonrefundable annual fee of $325 for all ejaculates stored and an additional $150 for the blood testing required by state law. A typical bill for conception, which takes roughly six once-a-month inseminations, using IUI, identity-release sperm with a photo match, is between $2,345 and $2,945. This price does not include the doctor's visits, ovulation predictor devices, or fertility medications and is generally not included under any insurance plans. Furthermore, many women attempt insemination twice during each ovulatory cycle, which would double the price of the conception bill.

Most banks also provide services for semen analysis, which is rec-ommended when using a directed donor (a man that a woman or cou-ple identifies as a potential donor). Semen analysis with a test that thaws frozen semen to assess its survival is $160. A sperm count runs $70. Sperm banks also offer blood testing for $280, urine culture for cy-tomegalovirus testing (CMV) (required only if the CMV blood test is positive) for $100, and urine culture for gonorrhea and chlamydia test-ing for $220. There are optional genetic tests such as Tay Sachs carrier status for $150, cystic fibrosis carrier status for $150, and hemoglobin electrophoresis carrier status (for sickle cell anemia and thalassemia) for $55 (these tests are required if sperm will be shipped to New York State).

Why so many tests, and are they all necessary? A reasonable issue to consider is when these test options cross the line from providing im-portant information about a potential donor into exploiting the fears of those in need. But, then again, you can never be too careful when it comes to the well-being of your potential child—or can you? Tests pro-duce all types of information constructed as vital to the customers' decision-making process. Of course, like any corporation, most sperm banks want to maximize sales and profit, and one way to achieve that is to provide many diverse services.

As of May 2005, the FDA, which oversees and regulates the donation of cells and tissues (e.g., eyes, blood, organs, semen), adopted new rules to restrict gay sperm donors, despite the absence of any significant scien-tific reason. The rules recommend that "any man who has engaged in ho-mosexual sex in the previous five years be barred from serving as an anonymous sperm donor."[16] Such rules would make it impossible for a sexually active gay man to serve as a donor. This AIDS hysteria can be al-leviated by the available standard testing procedures, but, unfortunately, these proven scientific tests to rule out HIV are not sufficient when it comes to men who have sex with men. Leland Traiman, director of a clinic in Alameda, California, that seeks gay sperm donors has responded to the new regulations by stating, "Under these rules, a heterosexual man who had unprotected sex with HIV-positive prostitutes would be OK as a donor one year later, but a gay man in a monogamous, safe-sex rela-tionship is not OK unless he's been celibate for five years."[17] As sociolo-gist Steve Epstein argues in his history of the beginning of the AIDS epi-demic, the process of scientific inquiry is often bogged down by ideolog-ical biases that disable scientists and policy makers from rational action.[18] For policy makers, apparently, gay men just aren't careful enough.

Semen banks have also attempted to expand their markets using the internet. This new venue offers "high-tech" fertility services such as sex preselection procedures, where semen is manipulated in a lab to increase the likelihood of a baby of a particular sex. ZyGen Laboratories of Van Nuys, California, "Your Partner in the Cycle of Life," offers sex selection for $460 on fresh semen and $520 on frozen semen. Three of the largest and most popular semen banks—the California Cryobank, the Sperm Bank of California, and the Fertility Center of California—have their own websites for browsing donor catalogues and promotional materials.[19] With the click of a mouse, you can construct, search for, and order a downloadable dream daddy.

With the Danish Cryos International Sperm Bank, semen has gone global:

> Today, we deliver sperm related products to clinics or distributors in nearly 50 countries and donor semen to clinics in more than 40 countries. Cryos may be described as the largest sperm bank in the world with more than 200 donors available and 10,000 units of semen distributed each year resulting in about 1,000 pregnancies.[20]

With distribution networks across continents, semen travels across the information and reproductive superhighways. In addition to more lax regulations for this Danish semen bank, there is also a large international demand for strapping, blue-eyed, blond-haired donors. While semen banks still rely on hard copy advertising strategies, internet sites offer a component of user-driven, interactive decision making. Using the variables depicted on the California Cryobank's website, individuals are encouraged to concoct a dream daddy composed of the most desirable characteristics imaginable. Of course, this individual's sperm may not be available, but the website entices us to fantasize about that perfect semen sample to produce a gifted, attractive, and healthy baby.

It is not just sperm that are traded on the gamete market. Egg donation is increasing in popularity, but the risks, payment, and methods of retrieval are vastly different from those of sperm donation. Egg donation involves egg retrieval through a minor medical procedure called transvaginal ovarian aspiration. Eggs are sucked out of ovaries with needles inserted through the vaginal wall. There are risks of "hyperstimulation." Many women experience hot flashes, vaginal dryness, fatigue, sleep problems, body aches, mood swings, breast tenderness,

Table 1. Comparison Between Egg and Sperm Donation

	Egg Donation	Sperm Donation
Preparation	• Health screening • Psychological screening • Fertility drugs to stimulate ovaries (oral and injected)	• Health screening • Semen analysis • Masturbation once or twice per week at a semen bank
Risks	• Multiple health risks	• No physical health risks
Payment to donor	• $5,000–50,000 per retrieval[a]	• $60–100 per ejaculate[b]
Cost to recipient	• Drugs, IVF, and donor compensation start at around $20,000 and vary widely from clinic to clinic.	• Vials run between $250 and $400 and up with additional tests and procedures.
Ideal candidate	• The ideal egg donor is a healthy female between the ages of 21 and 31. While not mandatory, it is preferable that the candidate has had at least one healthy pregnancy prior to donation. • Anecdotal evidence also suggests there is a market for "Ivy League" eggs.	• The ideal sperm donor is a healthy male between the ages of 21 and 35. • Anecdotal evidence suggests that the inventory of taller men who are blond and blue eyed is most popular. Also, identity release donors are more desirable.
Regulation of industry	• Food and Drug Administration • American Society for Reproductive Medicine has developed guidelines for egg donation • American Association of Tissue Banks	• Food and Drug Administration • U.S. Public Health Service • American Association of Tissue Banks

a. Five to twenty eggs, sometimes more, can be retrieved. The fee is not based on how many eggs are retrieved.
b. It is possible for an ejaculate to be divided into up to three vials for cryopreservation. Also, many semen banks have a clause that states: "If the numbers of motile sperm are within our acceptance standards, you will be paid."

headache, or vision problems. A very small number of women experience severe ovarian hyperstimulation syndrome (OHSS), which can cause serious medical complications, including blood clots, kidney failure, fluid buildup in the lungs, and shock. In rare cases, hospitalization is necessary and the condition can be life-threatening. One or both of the ovaries may have to be removed. The risk of OHSS decreases after the eggs are retrieved. As a means of comparison, I present a table of differences between egg and sperm donation (table 1).[21]

Due to the retrieval methods and hormonal manipulation, it is easier both practically and emotionally to donate sperm than eggs. Annual estimates place the number of children born from donor semen at about

30,000 a year, and more babies are born in the United States from using semen donation than from in vitro fertilization (IVF).[22] But as semen banks multiply, they are not met with universal appreciation.

The threat some men seem to be experiencing by the creation, success, and even proliferation of semen banks is likely to be exacerbated by a recent trend reported in the *New York Times* in an article entitled "First Comes the Baby Carriage," which explores the burgeoning community of mostly heterosexual single mothers by choice.[23] Single mothers by choice are defined by the media, politicians, and themselves as different from unwed mothers. Typically, unwed mothers are stereotypically defined as teenage girls who get pregnant without being married. These types of mothers are a perennial concern of conservative politicians and are defined as a drain on national resources.[24] Unwed mothers may wish to have fathers more involved in raising their children. For a variety of reasons, some women choose to not have male mates or husbands. Single mothers by choice are often frustrated by the lack of eligible heterosexual male partners with a mutual interest in parenting. Also, there are obvious age differences between the two groups, as well as latent class differences. The national community-based organization, Single Mothers by Choice, provides the following definition:

> A single mother by choice is a woman who *decided* to have or adopt a child, knowing she would be her child's sole parent, at least at the outset. Typically, we are career women in our thirties and forties. The ticking of our biological clocks has made us face the fact that we could no longer wait for marriage before starting our families. Some of us went to a doctor for donor insemination or adopted in the United States or abroad. Others accidentally became pregnant and discovered we were thrilled.[25]

As the *Times* reporter discovers, "On the Internet, Ms. Carr discovered hundreds of pregnant single women trading notes. Some were arranging to send one another their leftover sperm." Indeed, in October 2005, the National Center for Health Statistics, an agency of the Centers for Disease Control and Prevention, issued a press release to report that births to unmarried U.S. women set a record, with increases being driven by unmarried mothers in their late 20s, particularly those 25 to 29. This press release was picked up by most news outlets and was continuously reported in fairly sensational ways. Medical news distributors disseminated the National Center for Health Statistics Report with the following headline: "Unmarried U.S. Women Delivered Record 1.47M Infants in 2004, Report Says."[26] *USA Today* reported, "Feds: 1.5 Million Babies Born to Unwed Moms in '04,"[27] and *Fox News* scrolled, "The birth rate for unmarried women hit an all-time high last year," continuously during its morning newscast on November 2, 2005.

The growth of single mothers by choice leads to some men fearing that participation in reproduction is being reduced to the anonymous and disembodied use of their sperm with no further rights to the baby once it is conceived. Indeed, there is a certain logic as the restoration of paternal rights extends from the existing activism of some men who claim paternal rights in abortion cases and advocate the transformation of custody laws; these groups claim to be working for the rights of bio-logical fathers, and they promote policies in which sperm is recognized as the exclusive property of the male who produces it. Such reactions led me to consider how the possibility of creating a "downloadable dream daddy" further exacerbates the current crises in masculinity.

Sperm banks have challenged traditional conceptions of father-hood and masculinity by removing men from the reproductive process, retaining just their sperm as proxy. Ironically, sperm banks also rein-force a number of hegemonically masculine ideals by excluding certain men and their sperm altogether. Semen banks emerged based on a pro-heterosexual family mandate to address male fertility concerns, yet some men (gay men, short men, men who are ill or disabled) are now discouraged from using semen banks. From the start, sperm banking has shifted the population it serves and the types of families it creates. Sperm banks market the chance to rematerialize, reconstitute, and re-produce the ideal (male) body. In order to be successful as a business en-terprise, sperm banks represent their product, semen, as simultane-ously a part of the body, a potential body, and a series of genetic codes. Sperm banks and consumers co-construct the desirable donor, the de-sired child, and the best raw material for the job. In turn, what is ad-vertised is a collaboration between the sperm bank and the consumer: the vial of supercharged, amplified, technologically enhanced, and germ-free sperm is a stand-in for a particular man embedded in specific lifestyle of health, fitness, education, and breeding which will result in a healthy, attractive, and intelligent child.

Physicians, health officials, and politicians together preserve the male status quo by creating policies and procedures that disable certain men from participation in semen banking. For example, driven by either state regulation or market forces, men who are of short stature (below 5 feet 10 inches), men who are high school dropouts, or men who have had sex with men are not allowed or encouraged to donate to many sperm banks. Implicitly, the body of the donor becomes encoded as genetic information. Do new products enable the best semen to rise to the occasion, or do popular and industry renderings of male factors of infertility generate anxiety about sperm and thus market demand for more expensive products and procedures?

TECHNOSEMEN

"Technosemen" is the latest new and improved bodily product that semen banks market to clients. These are technical, medical, even mystical processes that are carefully presented to potential clients and described in great detail. For instance, as discussed earlier, semen analysis includes sperm counts, morphology, motility testing, functional testing, and performance testing ranging from the swim-up methods to percoll and retrograde. As stated above, each test is accompanied by a price tag. In addition to semen analysis, which purports to be a method of ensuring "fertability" of the product, semen undergoes disease and genetic testing to diminish possible fears of genetic or contagious conditions such as AIDS. These strategies of semen analysis and disease testing create what I call "technosemen."

Marketing technosemen can challenge the assumed inelasticity of the semen market by convincing, or better yet guaranteeing to, the general public that technosemen is fertile, uncontaminated, and genetically "engineered" for desirable traits.[28] In this age of epidemics, cloning, and increased risk of environmental disasters, semen banks can capitalize on their low-tech procedures and increase their revenues. In so doing, semen banks participate in, reinforce, and bolster the public's fear about these material threats to the human race. Both semen banks and consumers would like to believe in the fantastic potential of this technosemen. "People come to us because they want the best possible sperm for their future offspring," one semen bank administrator told me. "We don't offer the village idiot, because we don't get much demand for such."[29]

The processes by which technosemen is produced and advertised to consumers are deeply connected with how the "contents" of the semen are stylized. Donor catalogues also help control women's choices regarding reproduction. Rather than using a turkey baster or having sex with a partner, women are encouraged to chart their ovulation, strip down in sterile white rooms, lie down on a table, put their feet in stirrups, and allow a physician to place frozen pellets as close to the cervix as possible. This procedure is not very painful. However, when using IUI-washed semen, a health-care provider inserts a catheter inside a woman's cervix and injects the semen past the cervix. Many report this to be a more painful procedure than ICI. IUI is also more effective at achieving pregnancy since the sperm are placed closer to the egg.

Three types of information about technosemen are highlighted by semen banks: phenotypic characteristics (including race or ethnicity, hair color, skin tone, eye color, height, and weight), biological characteristics (including blood type, RH factor, and bone size), and social characteristics (including years of education, occupation, and hobbies and interests). These divisions serve as ways to easily segment the market, but they also do much more. Semen banks prioritize differences that they believe are important to the client through the ordering of the characteristics of men.

Race or ethnic origin is one of the key categories presented. It is assumed as a starting point or primary choice as several lists are sectioned according to race. However, it is not clear that any racial group is marketed more strongly than another by semen banks. Most semen banks market semen from donors with a wide variety of racial and ethnic backgrounds. Anecdotal evidence suggests that most consumers prefer to buy semen from donors with racial characteristics that are similar to their own. Thus marketing of any one group or groups over others could prove costly to semen banks' bottom lines.

Social characteristics are usually presented toward the end of each list. Although they are not given as much significance as phenotype characteristics, they are presented as consequentially creating differences in semen. These differences imply that semen can indicate a donor who smokes, rides a motorcycle, or would work at a nuclear power plant. Thus the inheritance of acquired characteristics is assumed. This conditions the client's perception of the semen. As clients perceive semen as being invested with "important" social characteristics, it is in the semen banks' best financial interest to keep this belief supported. Also, by associating certain social characteristics with semen, semen banks imply genetic rather than environmental, thus intensely individual, bases for them. By the same token, social bases for behavior are implicitly underplayed. They do not list a man's political party, how he treats his mother, or whether or not he recycles.

In addition, men are categorized by their social and physical power. Height, weight, body build, and favorite sports provide indicators of a donor's health and ability to be physically dominant. Categories of occupation, grade point average, and years of college provide indicators of social survivability and social dominance. Largely missing from these catalogues are semen samples from donors who do not rate highly within these categories. Thus, these categories tend to reify the power differences among men.

While semen banks anthropomorphize semen across many different dimensions, they simultaneously reinforce certain nonhuman characteristics. For example, they construct semen as "agentic," as being able to act in different ways upon other entities. "Natural" or unprocessed sperm are constructed as irrational, dirty, and unpredictable.[30] They may cause genetic disaster. Of course, it is in the semen banks' best interest not to be too cavalier in constructing semen as having agency, free will, or consciousness because they ensure their own livelihood by making clients believe their product is better than natural semen. Ultimately, sperm banks reengineer technosemen as new and improved and thus superior to embodied, natural semen. In other circumstances, semen banks construct technosemen as more rational than "natural" semen or as "less risky" to women. Technosemen is able to create better children, who are taller, more talented, and smarter than those produced by "natural" semen. Semen banks are able to capitalize on consumers' concerns about the risks of producing a child with birth defects or even one who might be bullied in the schoolyard. Despite all of this, to my knowledge, there have been no scientifically valid studies proving that donor sperm is better than embodied sperm.

Gaining the competitive edge in semen banking has come to mean presenting the best donor catalogue, a catalogue that presents a large number of available donors with the most socially desirable traits. Technosemen, then, relies on actual men but improves on them and may even eliminate them from the process of reproduction and parenting altogether. But taking the actual man out of the picture has not gone unnoticed. In fact, I would argue that sperm banking and donor insemination have escalated the crisis in masculinity and the legitimacy of men as social beings.

Judging from the list of presidents, executive directors, and medical directors from the AATB, owners and operators of sperm banks are overwhelmingly male, and we could consider their role as surrogate fathers in the reproductive process. In this role, male prerogatives may have determined who may be a donor and who may not, which social and genetic characteristics are most appropriate within the semen they sell, and what the social relations of donors will be to the children produced with their "donations." While semen banks have the potential to radically open up control to women over their own bodies, to assist in the proliferation of alternative family structures, and to provide additional means for participating in the reproductive process to men, such promises are being significantly compromised by ideas about masculinity within the industry.

DADDIES STRIKE BACK

Mannotincluded.com (Man Not Included), a British sperm virtual marketplace, is the latest and, perhaps, most transparent of assisted reproductive sites. There is no mistaking the mission of this site as empowering women to reproduce without male partners. From their website:

> Single and lesbian women have been denied the opportunity of using artificial insemination and have had to resort to locating a donor via a friend or even advertising. Mannotincluded.com believe that it is every woman's right to have children if they so wish and that is why we operate the only fresh sperm donation service in the world that is open to any woman, be she single, lesbian or married. By choosing to go on the Man Not Included programme you will have access to hundreds of voluntary donors who have registered with us simply because they also believe in this right and

want to help. Donors are usually always available when contacted by us and will do their utmost to be flexible around the recipients' timescales.[31]

While the manipulation, marketing, and merchandising of sperm to serve clients' needs and desires is not new, and the promotion is truly transgressive to mainstream social and biological reproductive ideas,[32] this service boasts over 5,500 anonymous male donors and over 3,000 single women, heterosexual and lesbian, registered for potential matches and future inseminations. But the service has not been without controversy. Josephine Quintavalle, director of Comment on Reproductive Ethics (CORE), a public-interest group focused on ethical dilemmas about reproduction, urged: "The whole idea must be vigorously resisted and men must see this initiative for what it is—yet another attack on their role in society. The male must not be reduced to a vial of anonymous sperm, and the rights of children to enjoy real fathers must be protected."[33] This panicky comment claims that men must be protected from an ongoing attack of their annihilation from families and "society" and that "real fathers" (read: biological) are superior to other types of parents. Clearly, the 5,500 men who have participated as anonymous donors in Man Not Included (in addition to thousands of sperm bank donors) have a different take on the notion of paternity and their "role in society." These comments seem ironic, however, given the notion that "papa was a rolling stone," through which men have opted out of fatherhood for centuries. As the construction goes, their role is to spread their seed but not take care of their kids, thus leading to the term "deadbeat dad."

Currently, through sperm banking or unprotected heterosexual intercourse either with men's consent or without their knowledge, men's sperm can be collected or used. Women who want to have children can bypass a man's future involvement by purchasing their semen or "tricking" male sex partners into "donating" it. Women's self-determination, a perpetual problem for male-dominated societies, is underscored when men are rendered "only good for one thing." Ironically, the technological innovation that enabled men who were infertile to participate in reproduction is now used to eliminate certain

Figure 5.2. On Father's Day in 1997, as part of a promotion, Absolut Vodka enclosed 50,000 free ties with copies of the *New York Times* Sunday edition. The title of the campaign was "Absolut Dad." Using the company logo, an Absolut bottle, and adding a tail, the blue tie is covered in sperm. From *New York Times*.

men from the reproductive process. Men do not seem to be taking this lying down, as an advertisement for Absolut Dad seems to indicate (figure 5.2).

In the Western world in the 1970s, as a response to second-wave feminism, men's groups emerged to advocate for a better understanding of men's roles in society, of the meaning of masculinity, and the reality of sexism—politicking for gender neutrality in court custody cases was one of the platforms of some men's rights groups. Today, the fallout can be seen in the rhetoric of many men's movement groups who directly blame feminists (a seemingly monolithic group) for the rise of semen banking. According to this logic, feminists, universally, saw men merely as sperm donors and not as fathers. The Fatherhood Responsibility Movement (FRM) emerged in the 1990s as a loose coalition of men's groups in the United States, including the National Fatherhood Initiative, Institute for Responsible Fatherhood and Family Revitalization, and National Practitioners Network for Fathers and Families. The FRM emerged alongside the introduction of new sperm technologies.

There are two wings of the FRM: those members interested in reversing the deterioration of conditions that support families, or "fragile families," as they are called; and those members interested in strengthening heterosexual, state-sanctioned marriages, those that are "pro-marriage." Both rely on fairly traditional heterosexual renderings of masculinity. The fragile family wing maintains that low-income and minority families are at a disadvantage in maintaining active fathers and works to establish programs that combat poverty, joblessness, and racism. The pro-marriage wing sees feminism as diminishing the moral obligation of fathers and advocates for heterosexual marriage as a moral valence for keeping fathers involved with their families. Even President George W. Bush and his administration have gotten involved, with two policy plans: the Responsible Fatherhood Initiative for community and faith-based organizations to provide training to keep fathers involved emotionally and financially, and the Healthy Marriage Initiative for research into ways to keep marriages strong. There are no such initiatives or policies to support single motherhood, gay fathers, or gay and lesbian families.

On the pro-marriage side, David Blankenhorn, founder and president of the Institute for American Values, helped create the National Fatherhood Initiative (NFI) in 1994. He serves as chairman of that organization's board of directors. Another founder of the NFI, Don Eberly, is a former Bush administration deputy director of the White House Office of Faith-Based and Community Initiatives. Since 1994, the NFI has had high visibility in the United States through public campaigns; policy initiatives on the local, state, and federal levels; and expanded research agendas. As part of a public awareness campaign, the NFI distributes public service announcements advertising fatherhood. For example, in their poster, "What It Takes," the NFI explains the difference between being a father, depicted as a sperm cell under a microscope, and being a dad, depicted by a list of activities.

Blankenhorn's group and other self-identified segments of the men's and fatherhood rights movements have appropriated the rhetoric of a supposed "fatherhood lost" to create spurious social psychological correlations between a child's lack of relationship to his or her biological father and supposed negative outcomes for that child. FRM proponents claim that paternal deprivation leads to individual pain, in the form of children's drug abuse and teen pregnancy, as well as collective societal suffering, in the form of higher crime rates and greater welfare expenses. Specifically, the website for the NFI composes a list of "Father Facts," including, "Children who live absent their biological fathers are, on average, at least two to three times more likely to be poor, to use drugs, to experience educational, health, emotional and behavioral problems, to be victims of child abuse, and to engage in criminal behavior than their peers who live with their married, biological (or adoptive) parents."[34] This correlation is a false one. It is not single motherhood but poverty and parental conflict (in separated and intact families) that have been demonstrated to lead to poor outcomes in children's mental health and social adjustment.[35] Through misconstruing and manipulating research findings, the FRM (through organizations like the NFI) do not critically investigate solutions to the economic, social, and personal obstacles that would disable men from becoming competent and compassionate fathers. Rather, through media spin, there is a construction of cultural bias, or conspiracy, against fathers that strips them of their rights, thus creating massive social problems.

Clearly, paternal deprivation is also tacitly used to state how men experience loss from being denied the ability to be fathers. In most studies of custody battles after divorce, men self-report feelings of depression and hopelessness with respect to their relationship to their children. Throughout the past 10 years, Blankenhorn's NFI has spearheaded a campaign to provide public service announcements, as well as helped form both the Congressional and the Senate Task Forces on Responsible Fatherhood in an effort to raise awareness and create policies to promote healthy fatherhood and create father-friendly legislation.[36] At a conference for the Danish Institute for Human Rights on June 2, 2005, Blankenhorn outlined his group's manifesto, "The Rights of Children and the Redefinition of Parenthood," which states, "Every child has the right to a natural biological heritage, defined as the union of the father's sperm and the mother's egg." The NFI is relentless in its portrayal of father absence as the propeller that drives all domestic social problems.

Accurately measuring the state of fatherhood is a difficult proposition. Marriage rates are not a good indicator of fatherhood since many couples choose to have children without getting married, and many divorced men are active fathers. Importantly, there are also connections between the federal government and those who lament the supposed decline of fatherhood. In 2000, Wade Horn, a previous president of the NFI and the Health and Human Services assistant secretary for children and families, wrote multiple articles on fatherlessness, such as "Save the Dads," in which he queries, "Will fathers become extinct in the next century?"[37] Recently, Horn was identified as providing syndicated columnist Maggie Gallagher with federal contracts in the amount of $21,500 while she was also writing columns that supported the Bush administration's $300 million initiative encouraging marriage as a way of strengthening families. Both President and Mrs. Bush have repeatedly pushed the idea of "fatherhood restoration." As President Bush put it at the Fourth National Summit on Fatherhood in 2001, "A child's greatest source of security today is not only knowing 'my mom loves me' and 'my dad loves me,' but also that Mom and Dad love each other. If we are serious about renewing fatherhood, we must be serious about renewing marriage."[38] Laura Bush added at the National Fatherhood Initiative awards gala on April 19, 2005, "Celebrating fatherhood is something our whole society should be doing."[39]

Cultural anxiety about fatherhood is expressed in the news media with stories from *U.S. News and World Report* like "Promoting No-Dad Families: Artificial Insemination and Single Women." Reporter John Leo believes David Blankenhorn has tapped into the social problem of fatherlessness encouraged by selling semen to single women: "Biological fatherhood was once understood by society to carry with it permanent moral obligations to the child. Now it can involve nothing more than a financially strapped college student masturbating into a cup for $50 and writing a vaguely caring letter to an offspring he will never see or care about."[40]

Certain men's groups have worked to establish social mores that reinforce fatherhood. Many sociologists and journalists, including Michael Kimmel, the author of *Manhood in America*, and John Stoltenberg, the author of *Refusing to Be a Man*, question the hidden assumption of these policies.[41] For example, Kimmel has written:

> Men's movement leaders speak to men not as fathers but as sons searching for their fathers. But curiously, the attendees at the workshops are middle aged men, many of whom are themselves, fathers. . . . They speak as sons, of their pain as sons estranged from fathers. That is, they would rather complain about something they can barely change than work towards transforming something they can: their relationships with their own children and the structured inequities of power between men and women, adults and children, and between one man and another.[42]

Trish Wilson, a blogger and freelance journalist, has been quite pro-
lific in writing about her investigations of the rise of fatherhood rights
movements. She points out that while the Responsible Fatherhood Project, operating under the auspices of the Department of Health and
Human Services, provides federal funding funneled through state governor's offices to fathers and fatherhood groups, mothers and family
forms outside heterosexual married couples do not get similar, positive
support from the government. She writes:

> "Fatherlessness" is the code-word for "single mother-headed house-
> holds," which are both blamed and condemned for allegedly creating
> social pathology. The real concern for Horn, Blankenhorn, and Pope-
> noe as well as men's and fathers' rights advocates is not the desire for
> men to become better, more responsible parents. They are reacting to
> the relinquishment of certain aspects of power and privilege that het-
> erosexual men have enjoyed in the context of the traditional, wedded,
> nuclear family. What we are seeing is a concerted effort to restore the
> dominance of the heterosexual nuclear family through governmental
> initiatives and fathers' rights-initiated restructuring of family law as a
> reaction to a perceived loss of male power and privilege.[43]

Blakenhorn explores the different "cultural scripts," what I
would define as social expectations taught to us until they become
automatic, of various types of fathers, from deadbeat dads to stepfa-
thers, but the chapter of most relevance here is one entitled "The
Sperm Father":

> The Sperm Father completes his fatherhood prior to the birth of his
> child. His fatherhood consists entirely of the biological act of ejacula-
> tion. He spreads his seed, nothing more. He is a minimalist father, a
> one-act dad. Neither a New Father nor an Old Father, he is an unfather,
> leaving no footprints or shadows. . . . His is the fatherhood of the one-
> night stand, the favor for a friend, the donation or sale of sperm.[44]

Blankenhorn suggests that it is only through "healthy" heterosexual marriage that good fatherhood is possible. The sperm father is thus
highly problematic for the development of good children and a good
society. Sperm fathers threaten the core notions of fatherhood and can
topple fathers' position in a society. As Blankenhorn writes, "to make

room for the Sperm Father is also to insist upon the essential irrelevance of all fathers"; this sperm father reduces the role of father to merely one-shot contributor of gametes. Furthermore, he argues that sperm fathers single-handedly create dreadful, social situations for many generations: "A society of Sperm Fathers is a society of fourteen-year-old girls with babies and fourteen-year-old boys with guns."[45]

According to Blankenhorn, the creation of sperm fathers is a post-modern phenomenon and an outgrowth of capitalism. It becomes obvious fairly quickly that what Blankenhorn finds morally objectionable is the creation of nonheterosexual families and not the actual use of donor semen. He indicates that it is morally acceptable for sperm to be sold to infertile couples, but that the growing use of this sperm for unmarried women is detrimental to society. Indeed, his 12 points for social change include the following as number 10:

> State legislatures across the nation should support fatherhood by reg-ulating sperm banks. New laws should prohibit sperm banks and oth-ers from selling sperm to unmarried women and limit the use of arti-ficial insemination to cases of married couples experiencing fertility problems. In a good society, people do not traffic commercially in the production of radically fatherless children.[46]

Consistent with the moral panic about what constitutes a "good so-ciety," selling sperm to women without enforcing attachment to men is a threat to children's well-being. Beckoning the legislature to step in to regulate sperm banks, Blankenhorn wants to establish strict rules on who should reproduce and how, what types of families are acceptable, and who makes the "best" children. Blankenhorn's views are clearly among the most extreme of those who object to the growing reliance on sperm banks. Still, one policy implication under consideration at the NFI is instituting state laws that require mothers to identify both mari-tal and nonmarital fathers on birth certificates.

Responding to technological innovations that create sperm cells as commodities, people are adjusting to sperm's new potentials. There-fore, it is important to consider the model ideas of family and parent-hood that Blankenhorn suggests, particularly since he suggests social policy. By linking the creation of an ethically superior society ("a good society") with said society's restriction of sperm to certain acceptable individuals, Blankenhorn seems to suggest the transformation of sperm into a state-controlled substance that should only be available to certain state-sanctioned citizens.

I would not argue that children do not need fathers. Personally, I feel the more adults in a child's life who love and care for him or her, the better. What I find most troubling, at times even Orwellian, about NFI and Blankenhorn's advocacy for fatherhood rights, is the ways in which they portray fatherhood as "in jeopardy." Proposing policies that control and limit the use of human sperm is an attempt to wrest power away from certain groups of people—in particular, women. Furthermore, the continued restricting of what or who gets to count as a father—namely, the monolithic version of a heterosexual, married provider who biologically reproduced a child—only exacerbates the problem of finding a workable way to parent in an increasingly hectic world. Clearly, some men are in pain about their disconnection from their children and families. But blaming semen banking, lesbians, and single mothers for the lack of sustained paternal involvement is not a solution. This type of scapegoating is a tactic that disables men from examining the reasons they might not be fully integrated into families or marriages in the first place. It's also worth noting that according to the U.S. Department of Health and Human Services, 68 percent of child support cases were in arrears in 2003, an increase from 1999 when it was 53 percent.[47]

SHOOTING BLANKS OR SHOOTING BANKS

Although semen banking threatens actual men with respect to their beliefs about fatherhood and paternal deprivation, semen banking has also facilitated progressive social change. While the liberating potential of semen banking for women cannot be underestimated, fatherhood is being reconstituted. The forces of capitalism and masculinity are encroaching on traditional fatherhood and enabling a myriad of options to be imagined and achieved: gay daddies, blended gay families, father-figures that many lesbian and single women recruit to be part of their children's lives. At the same time, reproductive professionals are attempting to wrest control of reproductive processes from women by creating barriers to their direct purchase of semen. At present, semen banks rarely send their products directly to consumers. Rather, due to both medical restrictions and fear of litigation, either the semen is sent to consumers' physicians or insemination procedures are carried out at the banks themselves.

While the fatherhood rights movement can be fairly easily deconstructed as a nostalgic and neoconservative attempt to reassert male dominance in the family, certain other effects of semen banking have implications for masculinity and men's lives. Even though women and men are often asked to measure up to a monolithic male gold standard, we should develop other standards to understand masculinity. Consumers are encouraged to believe that social characteristics are genetically encoded in semen. Importantly, semen banks market donor characteristics—such as body build, grade point average, height, and sports activities—which reinforce traditional notions of what it means to be a man. These characteristics rank men across strata of social and physical power. In choosing men who rank highly across these categories, both women and semen banks are tacitly supporting traditional ideas of masculinity and thereby reproducing existing gender relations. Thus, semen banks may limit the abilities of large numbers of men to participate in these alternative types of procreation. How semen banks broker their commodities is shaped by how we think about men, which, in turn, influences our future understandings about men.

In the age of sperm banks, what can be made of the reformulation of fathers? There are multiple groups each with a stake in reformulated fatherhood in the 21st century. As illustrated by the *New York Times* articles that began this chapter, some children conceived from anonymous semen donors want to know their donors and understand the connections between themselves and these men, genetic and beyond. There is also a vocal and authoritarian segment of politically organized men who appear to desire a nostalgic version of fatherhood and are clearly resistant to the "advances" of the reproductive technological imperative. Perhaps certain groups of men wish to get back to the land or return to "the natural" way, where we needed to get semen directly from its source instead of all this high-tech nonsense.

But now women can use the technological commodity of technosemen to their advantage. Enabled by their economic buying power, certain women are creating an inversion of old gender dichotomies by purchasing technosemen. Historically, these dichotomies have represented men as more rational and scientific beings, whereas women were thought to be more irrational beings or closer to nature. Think of the concepts of "women's intuition" and mother earth as opposed to "men of science or enlightenment" and "The Thinker," which is a man.[48] Women have long been associated with a more irrational or hysterical temperament and, as such, have been thought to be unfit for much of what society has to offer: politics, business, the military, and athletics come to mind. In an ironic twist on these old chestnuts, women can now use the rational technology for their own ends by extracting sperm from the male body and men, at least certain men, seem to be the "hysterical" ones, claiming they are no longer needed.

6

The Little Bit Left Behind

Semen as Evidence

According to many survivors of sexual assault and criminal investigators, DNA is powerful and decisive:

> I was raped in 1994, and in April of 1997, I was called by the detective who was working my case down to the police station. She showed me a picture of the rapist and I asked how did she know. She said, "DNA tells us." To this day, the only reason I know what the rapist looks like is because DNA tells me. . . . Since then, I have become a huge crusader of DNA. I love DNA—it is our friend. Because DNA can do so much. It identifies the bad guy; it tells us who is committing these crimes.[1]

Historically, female bodies have been considered "leaky," menstrual blood and breast milk being the most obvious examples.[2] Men are now being seen in similar terms; seminal emissions are unpredictable, making male bodies subject to leaks. No matter how valiant the effort made to contain and control semen, the substance is messy. As a result, adolescent boys have furtively changed their sheets, women and girls have become pregnant accidentally, diseases have been transmitted even during "protected" sex, and semen has been left behind, on or inside bodies or on clothes, at the scene of a crime. In other words, regardless of an individual man's intent, semen can leak into and onto bodies, sheets, and articles of clothing. It can also leak out of bodies—a process known as flowback in forensic circles—and leave resilient stains, or spill over onto someone else's clothing.

At first a mysterious and mythical substance, today semen can be both demystified and obscured by biological science, particularly forensics. With exacting specificity, scientists have labored to measure and interpret each sensory dimension of semen (color, taste, odor, consistency, shape, size, and volume). Through the advent of DNA technologies, sperm cells are used as the ultimate identifier in sexual crime scene investigations. More than a key piece of evidence, though, sperm has emerged as a proxy for female testimony about male sexual actions.

WARM STAINS, COLD HITS

Seminal discharges have become public property and are now indexed for posterity in the FBI's Combined DNA Indexing System, known as CODIS.[3] CODIS is a hierarchical, multilayered system of databases that compares DNA profiles for the purpose of linking crimes to other crimes or previously convicted offenders. Before CODIS, there were two classes of DNA casework: cases with a known suspect and cases without a known suspect. Through CODIS, there are no longer any cases with unknown suspects; instead, there are cases in which DNA is the suspect awaiting the revelation of identity. A forensic index contains DNA from crime scenes, and an offender index contains DNA profiles from convicted offenders and crime scenes at the local, state, and national levels in the United States. The ultimate goal and measure of success in forensic investigations is to produce a cold hit. A cold hit is a match between the computer forensic index and the offender index. The FBI's website states: "The FBI Laboratory's Combined DNA Index System (CODIS) blends forensic science and computer technology into an effective tool for solving violent crimes. CODIS enables federal, state, and local crime labs to exchange and compare DNA profiles electronically, thereby linking crimes to each other and to convicted offenders."[4] CODIS can be used to generate suspects in cases where there might not have been an obvious suspect based on witness testimony alone.

The advent of CODIS compels comparison to Michel Foucault's *The Birth of the Clinic* and *Discipline and Punish,* where he introduces us to the notion of a clinical gaze.[5] Foucault understands the clinical gaze as a tool for modern society to reveal, and thereby control and discipline, the "truth" of the body. That is, professionally trained experts armed with diagnostic technologies create systems for measuring, labeling, and ranking bodies. The clinical gaze becomes standardized through the creation of templates that ensure diagnostic reproducibility and limit subjective assessments. There are multiple clinical gazes that rank the mental and physical health and fitness of the human body. Examples include the body mass index (BMI), cholesterol levels (HDLs and LDLs), blood pressure, and sperm counts. These clinical gazes assume some desirable number that is equivalent to a desirable physical or mental trait; any deviation from the desirable number is considered a problem and often results in further testing. These numbers are also used in larger databases to determine trends in populations and policies for controlling these populations. These systems of standardization thus became means of social power and produce a socially controlling environment.

On an individual level, there are multiple ways the clinical gaze makes you feel "watched." During health-care interactions, a doctor can measure your BMI and announce that you are overweight. Or you might read the equation for BMI in a fitness magazine and discover you are overweight. Or you might have your BMI measured at the gym and be told you are overweight. The knowledge that you are overweight operates as a mechanism to bring your behavior back into the realm of what is socially desirable. Losing weight results in new numbers to be entered into the formula, which results in a lower BMI and a new understanding that you are "normal" weight.

On a societal level, the clinical gaze of genetic testing and genetic typing has enabled the innovation of CODIS as a system that extracts genetic data from evidence and uses this data to search the general population. CODIS produces another clinical gaze focused on human bodies and another way in which individuals can be watched, measured, and tracked. Through the processes of standardization, information about individual human bodies is aggregated to create a database for social control. In his work on prisons, Foucault likewise shows that certain types of men must be controlled because they are dangerous. Ultimately, the power of the clinical gaze is that it can naturalize "official" knowledge about ideas of normalcy, criminality, and insanity.

What seems to be emerging from the way CODIS is being used is the rise of a deeply interconnected medicalized criminal justice system and a decline in civil liberties for "potential" perpetrators. For example, the practice of pretext arrests—where the police profile individuals for arrest so that they can obtain a DNA sample—is one such consequence. In testimony from March 2000, before a House Judiciary Sub-Committee on Crime, Barry Steinhardt, who served as associate director of the American Civil Liberties Union between 1992 and 2002, cited a study from 1990 that revealed that 64 percent of drug arrests of whites and 81 percent of Latinos were not sustainable and 92 percent of black men arrested on drug charges were later released for lack of evidence or inadmissible evidence.[6] Those arrested but not convicted are required to give DNA samples in certain states. Many states are attempting to change these laws that will allow for the collection of DNA samples from all arrestees prior to conviction.

A pretext arrest is an example of what Troy Duster, a sociologist, calls a "functional creep."[7] Through the linking of databases, DNA identification technology intended to be used for exclusively violent criminals including murderers or rapists, is now able to hook up with other databases and "capture" individuals for petty crimes. The rapid expansion of systems such as CODIS have resulted in certain databases (or tools) created for a distinct purpose and scope, expanding into new functionality and applications as they are developed and merge with other systems over time. The ever-changing and expanding develop-ment of databases for criminal investigations reads like an Orwellian nightmare. The law enforcement and forensics database nexus begins with local databases of DNA collection linked to federal violent crime indices. Over time, the local databases are consolidated, or federalized, and linked with data from anyone convicted of criminal activity. A fur-ther shift associates a federal DNA database with data from those who have been arrested. Finally, DNA evidence is in some cases sufficient for pretext arrests.

The New York State Division of Criminal Justice Services' compre-hensive review of hits on the New York State DNA Data Bank lauds the CODIS system as having prescient functions:

> The principal utility of CODIS lies in its unprecedented contribution as an evidentiary tool in establishing (or eliminating) suspect identities in criminal investigations. However, on a much broader scale, CODIS of-fers the potential to prevent future crimes by expediting interventions earlier in the careers of criminals at risk of becoming high-rate offend-ers before their offending behavior can escalate and diversify.[8]

Since official forensic analysis and bureaucratic management is firmly situated in the medical/scientific/legal nexus, the knowledge it produces about human bodies appears to be very scientific, objective, and technically specific. Seminal fluid contains DNA, which is biomed-ical, rational, objective proof. However, since biases do exist within medicine, science, and law, and because there are power differentials between men, CODIS does not treat all male DNA evidence equally. Existing power relations and notions about masculinity inform the scientific treatment of semen. Higher-status men with money who can manipulate the criminal justice system through legal maneuvers are likely able to keep their semen out of CODIS. Ultimately, CODIS manages to extract semen and catches some men within the database, while others are set free.

Today, federal, state, and local crime scene investigators probe locations of seminal residue—sheets, clothing, underwear, vaginas, and rectums—and analyze their findings for DNA markers. Outside of government and law enforcement, others are capitalizing on the technological imperative of these innovations. Television programs focusing on sex crime investigations prominently feature cutting-edge DNA technologies. Not surprisingly, these shows don't specify the constraints of governmental (federal, state or local) budget shortfalls or their ability to use the latest state-of-the-art technology. Despite all the hype and use of sex crimes as a hook to get citizens to vote for tough crime laws and violations of privacy, in reality many rape kits are never processed due to expense and an often enormous backlog of cases.[9] There is also a growing market for at-home semen evidence collection kits to be used for personal sleuthing (i.e., checking the sheets or underwear of a supposedly unfaithful partner, or in a few cases, at least, a teenager[10]).

While I maintain a critical stance toward these forensic techniques, and, by extension, their construction of the male body as an entity that is subject to surveillance, the use of DNA forensics does have advantages. Clearly, DNA evidence can be useful in helping to identify and capture violent criminals. In addition, DNA evidence can also exonerate those who have been wrongly accused or imprisoned, as demonstrated by organizations like the Innocence Project.[11] However, the uncritical celebration and instititutionalization of DNA forensics has led rather quickly to practices such as DNA profiling that claim to identify DNA markers of some men who are dangerous, criminal, or violent.[12] Eerily similar to late-19th- through early-20th-century efforts to identify criminals based on physical characteristics like the "criminal skull" or the "criminal nose," the identification of the so-called criminal gene is a slippery slope where an assumption of guilt or criminal intent can exist without proof or evidence and, instead, be based on racial, ethnic, or similar associations.[13]

As sociologist Troy Duster has demonstrated, throughout the 20th century, there has been an increasing propensity to see crime, mental illness, and intelligence as expressions of genetic dispositions.[14] Duster draws on the troubling history of the eugenics movement to show how racial stereotypes and assumptions can often cloud or overshadow scientific or medical knowledge. In the case of semen, it is through the production, procurement, and description of forensic evidence that biomedical science gains entry to the criminal justice system by lending new credibility to the claims of law enforcement. This evidence can either incriminate or exonerate. However, there seems to be an endemic cultural lag as the social, moral, and legal interpretations of crime scramble to keep pace with biomedical innovation. This lag fuels confusion about biomedical practices, creates mistrust for investigators, and supports overconfidence in the irrefutability of physical evidence. The popularization of forensics in our vocabulary further complicates meanings about identity, individuality, evidence, guilt, crime, and confession. Simultaneously, as the forensic vernacular becomes more popular to the nonscientist, expectations about DNA are both glorified and oversimplified.

SULLIED BY SEMEN: HISTORICAL FOUNDATIONS

Current crime scene investigation uses different approaches to find semen. The two new popular methods are called "presumptive" and "confirmatory" tests. Presumptive tests include visual or physical inspection of the crime scene using an ultraviolet light, also known as Wood's Light, to make semen fluorescent. Once a substance is identified as semen, confirmatory tests use biochemical procedures to determine the presence of sperm cells.[15] Usually, confirmatory tests involve microscopic examination of fabrics and staining of the material to identify morphologically recognizable spermatozoa. For example, one technique, called a "Christmas Tree" stain, uses a smear of what is known as a "differential" stain to distinguish sperm cells from epithelial cells, cells that line the inner and outer surfaces of organs. After an investigator collects a stain with a swab and agitates the swab in a test tube, a smear is created and placed on a microscope slide. Two dyes are used to determine whether sperm cells are present. Sperm heads stain red, tails stain green. Today, spermatozoa are essential to the criminal investigation since the sperm head contains the DNA. Presumptive and confirmatory testing generally culminates in DNA testing. But how did sperm become forensic evidence in the first place?

Forensic science developed with the rise of Enlightenment thinking in the late 1600s. During this time, the ultimate arbiter of truth shifted from the realm of religion to that of science. Forensics evolved naturally within the new scientific paradigm as a means of investigation that could be corroborated by testimony and evidence. This environment proved ripe for the proliferation of inventions, many of which would facilitate the investigation of crime scenes. As I demonstrate below, early forensic investigators, through the use of scientific practices, bestowed the morality of man onto the quality and quantity of their semen. What becomes clear when reading the history of forensic sciences is an allegory in which men as scientists and semen as evidence work in tandem to uncover the Truth.

Early to Mid 1800s: Identifying Semen

Tracing the genealogy of sperm as evidence leads us back to 12th century England, where King Richard I established the Office of the Coroner. The coroner was responsible for recording all criminal matters and investigating causes of unnatural deaths. As the demand grew for investigation of unnatural deaths, coroners began asking physicians for assistance. The increased demand for physicians to be educated in investigative matters eventually led to the University of Edinburgh in Scotland establishing a department of legal medicine in the early 1800s. Toward the end of the 18th century, modern chemistry emerged as a valid science and led to discoveries that were applicable to crime investigation and detection. The use of experts in the courtroom was first documented at the end of the 18th century.

When the presence of spermatozoa was recognized as the essential characteristic of a seminal stain, semen obtained a legal value. In 1839, forensic physicians Mathiew Orfila and Henri-Louis Bayard established a means of methodological assessment of semen, and it began to be used as biomedical legal evidence. Prior to this, cases of sexual assault were determined by the expertise of midwives.[16] As the rising esteem of rational, medical doctors—nearly all male—grew, midwives' authority on these issues was challenged and eventually taken over by physicians.[17]

Orfila, a Spaniard best known for his work in toxicology, explored the characteristics of semen on fabric in the early 1800s. When linen is "sullied by semen," then diluted in water for microscopic inspection, spermatozoa become crumpled and separated to the point of not being recognizable. Orfila explained that the ideal time to examine spermatozoa is soon after ejaculation when semen is placed on a glass slide: "For, independent of their form, which resembles that of a tadpole, they execute very marked movements and in the extreme, one can pronounce, solely after the existence of animalculi of this form, that the solution submitted to this examination is semen, for they are not observed with the same characteristics in any other liquid."[18] Bodily secretions other than semen on fabrics (women's discharge, mucous, saliva) were distinguished from semen by odor, by coloring when exposed to heat (or lack of coloring), and by how quickly the fluid dissolved in different solutions. Orfila's tests were ultimately rejected because of poor results, and it was not until 1839 that Bayard provided the first reliable microscopic analysis of semen on fabrics.[19] Leaky semen could then be accurately identified.

Simultaneously, the biomedical production of "spermatorrhea," a term coined in the middle 1800s, is perhaps the first medical understanding of the male body's pathology of leaking semen. Western European physicians discovered, diagnosed, and treated this condition of excessive discharge of sperm (from ejaculation, nocturnal emissions, urination, or sweating) caused by what was then considered to be illicit or excessive sexual activity. The condition was thought to cause anxiety, nervousness, lassitude, impotency, insanity, or death. As historian Ellen Rosenman writes: "Semen was pathologized as the symbol of everything that is alarming about the body."[20] The male body's inability to contain itself despite a conscious intention to not leak led to surgical treatments such as cauterization, in which a hot iron is used to seal tissues, and the application of biomedical apparatuses such as the 1876 Stephenson Spermatic Truss, a pouch that tied the penis down, making erection impossible, and the toothed urethral ring, a sharp-pronged device that would prick the penis if it became erect. Men were seen as victims of their own fluids, potentially lacking self-control and unable to contain the boundaries of their bodies.

The Early 1900s: Semen as the Measure of the Man

Dr. A. Florence (1851–1927), a professor of medicine, created a standard for professionals to use in determining whether there is actually semen present at the scene of the crime. Florence described the fluid in 1896:

"Semen (seed) is a thick, viscous liquid, a bit flowing, of an odor sui generis called 'spermatic,' and which has been compared to flowers of a chestnut tree, shredded hoof, sawn ivory, flour dough, gluten, etc."[21] Florence further asserted a correlation between a man's semen and his sexual or moral practices:

> Its consistency is variable: thick, almost a gelatin, in a vigorous man after a long abstinence, it becomes very fluid, scarcely milky, in those who abuse venereal pleasures. In the first case, it is an opaque white, bordering on yellow or grey, almost pearly, clotted, non-homogeneous, because striations in an uncolored, transparent liquid, appearing dark by a phenomenon of refraction, engulf the masses of gelatin. In the second case, it is rather homogeneous, more or less milky, a little translucent. In a degree of even more considerable im-poverishment again, after several repeated acts of coitus in a short pe-riod of time, it is transparent and shows only a few small whitish points or striations; at the same time the spermatic odor becomes weaker and weaker and even null.[22]

By implying that semen becomes less strong and substantial when it is spilled or wasted, virility is tied here to the notion of strength and morality. Conversely, it is also implied that wasting sperm is a sign of moral shortcomings or outright deviance. This conflation of semen with the relative perversion of a man is not merely a historical relic; the idea appears repeatedly in popular representations, as discussed below.

The Mid-1900s: Sperm as Identifier of Individual Man

In the late 1800s, photographs of faces were used to capture the criminal's portrait. Alphonse Bertillon (1853–1914), a French identification bureau chief, refined the system by adding the unique physical aspects of the individual to create a record that would identify the criminal.[23] By using the uniqueness of individual skeletal variations, precise meas-urements were recorded in a system that is known as "anthropometry." These anthropometric measurements, along with verbal description of the criminal and any distinguishing marks of the body, were kept on record in a centralized police file. This was a significant advancement in providing a centralized database of criminals for criminal investigators, and the system was used primarily to capture repeat offenders and apply a more scientific approach to the process. The Bertillonnage *portrait parle*, or spoken portrait, combined with the use of stains as evidence, shifted criminal investigation from the use of eyewitness testimony to the use of physical evidence.

One of Bertillon's students was Edmund Locard. Locard's Exchange Principle is widely regarded as the cornerstone of forensic science. This principle, first articulated around 1910, is based on theories of the cross-transfer of physical evidence between individuals and objects. Criminals who leaked fluid could now be associated with crime scene locations, objects, and victims. Throughout the growth of forensics, the field became more substantiated as it was incorporated into law enforcement and into the popular imagination—think of literature such as the Sherlock Holmes mysteries and agencies such as the Federal Bureau of Investigation, established in 1905. Crime laboratories were established in France in 1910 and in California in 1923, and the FBI crime lab became operational in 1932.

In 1953, biochemist Paul Leland Kirk published *Crime Investigation*, one of the first texts in the field that encompasses both practice and theory. Building on Locard's transfer theory, Kirk likened the transfer evidence to a "silent witness," as he called it. Florence's "irrefutable accusing witness" was a precursor to Kirk's silent witness: "Wherever he steps, whatever he touches, whatever he leaves, even unconsciously, will serve as silent evidence against him. . . . The blood or semen that he deposits or collects—all these and more bear mute witness against him."[24] Kirk continues to speculate that the criminalist of the future may be able to identify perpetrators by the hair, blood, or "semen he deposited," which were probably unique to the individual. This recalls Florence's 1895 harbinger of the legacy of sperm as signifier of a criminal man. As Florence states:

> Blood abounds, it runs in the streets, a scratch makes it flow and a number of professions cannot be practiced without its blemish. It is not the same for seminal stains, whose presence in frequent cases has an absolutely precise significance and constitutes an irrefutable accusing witness. Their interpretation is extremely easy, for, rather often, the role of the expert consists in saying yes or no as to the presence of spermatozoa.[25]

According to Kirk, where the semen is found can provide important information about the criminal/perpetrator. He urges criminalists to check areas other than the vagina for semen because "concomitant perverted sex activity" may have accompanied the crime.[26] Such moralizing about the type of sex further establishes the normalization of certain types of sexual activities—heterosexual, certainly, and again, for reproductive purposes—and those that are not normal or "perverted."

Prior to DNA testing, Kirk notes that there were excellent indications that the morphology of spermatozoa may have been characteristic of the individual man. Not every individual's sperm are normal in appearance, and the "variations from normal take several directions. . . . Distribution of various abnormalities and deviations is quite constant and [that] a statistical summary may serve to identify the individual from whom the spermatozoa originated."[27] If it is not possible to identify the criminal, it may be possible to use deviations to exonerate him. Kirk details the analysis of semen stains on fabric and suggests that cloth should be teased apart to separate as much as possible, as sperm tend to be caught by cotton fibers and tenaciously retained. He suggests employing distilled water and diluted hydrochloric acid to soak an encrusted spermatozoa loose. Marveling at the tenacity of sperm, Kirk reports, "The spermatozoa are not dissolved or damaged by any of these solvents, being one of the most resistant of all biological structures."[28] Even though sperm are unique and strong and resilient, a scientist is able to outsmart, identify, and extract the sperm from fabrics and bodies.

Middle to Late 1900s: Rise of DNA

In 1911, deoxyribonucleic acid, or DNA, was discovered. But the world was transformed in 1953, when the Nobel Prize winners in physiology and medicine, James Watson and Francis Crick, unfolded the "secret of life" from the chemical structure of DNA. DNA opened new frontiers in science and medicine while also opening up a host of ethical, political, and religious issues. Today, the media suggest that the power of DNA lies in its status as a tracking device; we are encouraged to believe that DNA can trace our heritage, our intellect, our whereabouts, and our defects. Stories about smart genes, cancer genes, and criminal genes abound. We are told that 99.9 percent of every human being's genetic makeup is the same. DNA connects us all, yet it is used in forensics to identify and separate one of us from the rest.

In 1984, Alec Jeffreys discovered a truly individual-specific identification system and coined the term "DNA fingerprinting." This identification system was used for the first time for criminal investigation in 1986. DNA profiling made its formal entry into the world of forensics with a murder case in a small town near Leicester, England, where two girls had been raped and murdered. A teenage boy from the area confessed to the second murder and was arrested. Police, frustrated and eager to solve the case, asked Jeffreys to analyze the semen samples from both victims to verify the boy's guilt in both murders. The DNA profile verified that the same man had committed both crimes, but it was not the teenager who had confessed. The boy was the first person proved innocent by DNA typing. The investigation continued with a DNA-based manhunt that involved screening all local men within a certain age range and eventually led to a man who matched the DNA profile signature. The implementation of this DNA fingerprinting had substantiated semen as a silent witness.[29]

Up until the mid-1980s, identity testing was generally conducted using serological tests, which identified proteins present in the seminal fluid. This proved problematic because some men, about 20 percent of the male population, do not secrete proteins into their seminal fluid, and semen from such individuals could not be typed. There were several other problems with the old serological tests, and they are now considered fairly unreliable. Since 1988, DNA testing has been the gold standard, and a variety of DNA tests are available for typing the DNA contained in spermatozoa.[30] Of course, some men are "aspermic," whereas others have had a vasectomy, and semen from such men can be challenging to type, but some of the more powerful polymerase chain reaction (PCR)–based DNA typing methods can determine a type from few DNA-containing cells present in the seminal fluid (other than spermatozoa).[31] There are a great number of DNA tests currently available for forensic work.

But the gold standard is not fool-, or foul-, proof. And the presence of seminal fluid at a crime scene may be proof of identity but not of an individual man's guilt. Michael Lynch, an ethnomethodologist and scholar of science and technology studies, asserts,

> Any defense lawyer who does a minimally competent job will quickly point out that a "match" is not evidence of guilt. The association between matching evidence and certainty of identity was first established with fingerprinting, and with DNA evidence there is still a

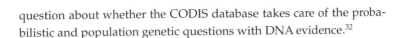

question about whether the CODIS database takes care of the probabilistic and population genetic questions with DNA evidence.[32]

Furthermore, within professional criminology circles, a new term, "the CSI effect," has been coined to describe phenomena in which actual investigators are responding to the expectations of millions of individuals who consume television crime show dramas. Jurors educated by television programs have come to expect a certain amount of forensic evidence in every trial.[33] So, as a good defense lawyer will point out, the presence of semen is not necessarily evidence of a crime because seminal fluid can leak out or be ejaculated without an act of assault or aggression. Nonetheless, jurors and the lay public tend to believe in the veracity of DNA evidence; indeed, as Owen Dyer, a journalist for the *British Medical Journal* reports, "enthusiasm for the technique has led to too much reliance being placed on it as a foolproof way to find the guilty man."[34]

LEAKS THAT BROUGHT DOWN A PRESIDENT AND A STAR SHOOTING GUARD, ALMOST

Scandal involving President Bill Clinton and intern Monica Lewinsky quickly introduced the "semen-stained blue dress" into everyday discourse. The transcript from the infamous *Starr Report*, published in 1998, establishes that leaked semen, mistaken for spinach dip, can be difficult to "spit out" or decipher. Even when it originates from high-status men, semen can be a messy substance. It is not easily contained and, when spilled carelessly, semen may be all the evidence required to implicate and indict individuals:

Q: So at the time you didn't notice anything on the dress?
ML: I don't believe so.
Q: Okay. What happened then the next time you wore the dress that led you to conclude that?
ML: Well, I also can I say here? I also—I think I wore the dress out to dinner that night, so which is why I'm not sure that that's what it is.
Q: Okay.

ML: So it could be spinach dip or something. I don't know. I'm
sorry could you repeat the question?

Q: Sure, when was the—when was it that you at least began to
believe that maybe there was semen on the dress?

ML: I really don't remember when it was the next time, I went
to wear the dress, but I gained weight so I couldn't wear the
dress and it didn't fit. And I'm not a very organized person.
I don't clean my clothes until I am going to wear them again.

Q: Did you notice there was something on the dress?

ML: Yes, and at that point I noticed it and I thought, oh, this is
dirty, it needs to get cleaned. And then I remembered that I
had worn it the last time I saw the President, and I believe it
was at that point that I thought to myself, oh, no.

Cultural critics see Clinton's spilled seed as a jolt to the nation, a
disruption to the social order through the immorality of semen leaking
during inappropriate sexual relations. The integrity of the Office of the
President was at risk, just as the integrity of the body of President Clinton escaped containment—Clinton was overcome by passion, and his
semen was the evidence of his transgression. Even debating the meaning of the word "is"—as in, that depends on what your definition of sexual relations is—could not obfuscate the physical DNA evidence of this
seminal stain. As Thomas Dumm, a political scientist, explains: "The
quasi-onanistic spilling of the seed signified something far more dis-
turbing to what we might call the image of the unified presidency,
namely that this president was in his weakness willing to part with his
precious bodily fluids."[35]

Just as sperm points to a unique man who ejaculated at the scene,
sperm is also used to encourage certain ideas about women. What can
sperm tell us about women? For example, a woman's claim of noncon-
sent is even more assiduously dismantled if her sexual encounter is
other than heterosexual, monogamous, and vaginal intercourse. The
difficult time basketball player Kobe Bryant's accuser has had since her
name was leaked out illustrates how famous and rich forensic semen is
like a scarlet letter for women. In the case of Bryant, an African American all-star NBA player, another man's sperm got him off the hook. In
2004, Bryant was accused of rape by a 19-year-old white woman with
whom he first denied, and then admitted to, having had sex. Bryant's
delayed admission was undoubtedly encouraged by the likelihood of

evidentiary seminal proof of his sexual violation—retrieved through a penile swab. Here are some excerpts from the transcripts of his interrogation with Colorado detectives Doug Winters and Dan Loya:

> Winters: OK. Um. I'll be blunt and ask you. Did you have sexual intercourse with her?
> Bryant: No.
> Winters: Yet there is an allegation that it was an unconsensual intercourse that occurred last night, OK. All right. Hang on, OK, hang on, I understand you have every right to be upset, OK, but you know, I'm giving you an opportunity to tell the truth if something did happen, because I'm going to tell you now, um, we're going to find out.

> ———

> Bryant: Is there any way I can settle this whatever it is, I mean . . . ?
> Winters: Well, what do you mean by settle?
> Bryant: If my wife, if my wife found out that anybody made any type of allegations against me she would be infuriated.

> ———

> Loya: Just be straight up, we're not going to tell your wife or anything like that. Did you have sexual intercourse with her?
> Bryant: Uh, this is what I need to know because uh I did have sexual intercourse with her. Cause I was (inaudible).
> Winters: And I understand.
> Loya: OK, was it consensual?
> Bryant: It was totally consensual.
> Loya: What makes you believe, what makes you believe it was consensual?
> Bryant: 'Cause she started kissing me, (inaudible) then she bent over and (inaudible).

> ———

> Loya: Is this, I don't mean to offend you in any way but is this a habit of yours, that you cheat on your wife?
> Winters: Has this ever happened before?
> Bryant: Um, yes, with one other person. And she could actually testify I do that um, I do the same thing, I hold her from the back, I put my hands (inaudible).

Loya: And who's that other person?

Bryant: Her name is Michelle.

Loya: And this is somebody you frequent or one time incident
    or . . . ?

Bryant: No. She's a, she's a frequent (inaudible).

Loya: And your wife . . .

Bryant: (Inaudible)

Loya: Obviously your wife doesn't know about this?

Bryant: No. Nothing man, seriously.[36]

Among the articles of clothing the accuser submitted to police for examination was a pair of underwear from the night she claims to have been raped. Later on, she went to the hospital for a sexual assault examination; at that time, she was wearing yellow underwear. That underwear was also taken from her by the nurses and, as well as the bagged evidence, submitted for forensic evaluation. Semen and sperm found in the yellow underwear did not match the DNA profile of Kobe Bryant. Therefore, it was surmised that the accuser who arrived at the hospital wearing underwear with someone else's semen and sperm in them had had sex with other men in addition to Kobe Bryant. The finding of this other spermatic evidence led to the decision to admit evidence of the woman's sexual activity in the 72 hours before her medical examination.

Among the frustrations suffered by the accuser, the court inadvertently posted her name and address on a website, as well as other confidential information, causing her to be hesitant to cooperate with prosecution. The negative public view that resulted from the ensuing media frenzy may have scared the victim. As an August 22, 2004, *New York Times* article states, "The Bryant case . . . has become part of an extended and tangled conversation about sexual assault, the boundaries of privacy and the power of celebrity."[37] Another man's leaked semen was Bryant's saving grace, enabling him to sway popular opinion and the courts' mercy. The yellow semen-stained underwear traced back to the other "donor" and weakened her claim of rape by portraying the accuser as more of a promiscuous opportunist than a victim. The media reports of these cases, as well as other high-profile or celebrity crime cases, often circulate around seminal evidence as reporters narrate in vivid detail where the semen was, how it was discovered, and to whom it belonged. So captivated is the popular imagination by seminal evidence, a whole genre of crime television offers seminal entertainment.

RIPPED FROM THE HEADLINES

Crime shows have generally fared well on network television. Fans still pay homage to shows like *Dragnet, Adam-12, Hawaii 5-0, Quincy, Hill Street Blues,* and *Homicide.* Since its debut in 2000, CBS's *Crime Scene Investigation (CSI)* has consistently ranked number one in television viewership.[38] Using a successful formula of biotechnical forensic practices, deductive reasoning, interpersonal drama, and grisly, slow motion reenactments, *CSI* has surpassed its competitors *NYPD Blue, Crossing Jordan,* and *Law and Order* (including *Criminal Intent* and *Special Victims Unit*). CBS network executives are so pleased with the show they have created two spin-off series, *CSI: Miami* and *CSI: New York,* as well as adding more crime shows like *Cold Case, Without a Trace,* and *Robbery Homicide Division.*

What can explain the fan base and mass appeal of these crime shows? As they stimulate, exploit, and generate fear, crime shows claim to reflect real life. *Law and Order's* storylines are often based on actual cases, hence the show's slogan "Ripped from the headlines." Most of the crime shows are really celebrations of the triumph of positive thinking. Amid all of the lies, deceptions, and partial evidence, these shows tell us week after week that the right deductive reasoning, testing, and fieldwork can reveal, with certainty, the criminal. These shows are locally produced but globally consumed. It is one of the many shows that exemplify the increasingly fuzzy boundary between reality and reality-based drama on television, as well as the boundaries between "reality" (actual grisly crimes quickly reported to a highly interested public) and the canon of crime fiction. Both genres are the dramatic grandchildren of Arthur Conan Doyle's Sherlock Holmes. Again and again on these shows, the discovery of semen at a crime scene automatically indicates and indicts a "very bad" man.

In these entertainment shows, women are generally portrayed as passive recipients of sperm. Indeed, on many crime shows, women are passive in the extreme—that is, they are dead. The rise of DNA forensics as practice and entertainment has recast women's bodies as an inert staging ground into which sperm gets deposited; women qua victims become crime scenes, or their bodies do, from which the "real" goods— the seminal samples—are swabbed. This representation as a passive repository evokes the world of straight porn, where women are simply holes for things to poke or spill into. Might the DNA sample be the forensic equivalent of the money shot? Women are props for seminal action: raping, ejaculating, policing, collecting, testing, prosecuting, examining, and proving. And as reality television continues to gain momentum, perhaps we will no longer rely on reenactments. Might we soon see actual dead woman's bodies as containers of seminal evidence?

Scriptwriters aren't the only ones getting ideas from the everyday lives of individuals. In 1998, after watching an *NYPD Blue* episode in which a rape victim saved the semen her attacker had left behind, a 12-year-old girl purposefully used a cotton swab on herself to gather sufficient DNA evidence to have her grandfather arrested. Interpreting the plot lines and transcripts from these programs, *CSI* figuring prominently among them, demonstrates the ways in which semen is both a silent witness and a go-to-guy in most criminal investigations.

It is important to note that in all these episodes, semen is invisible, discussed but never seen. Furthermore, semen will only bear witness for those with enough expertise to draw out its testimony. The crime shows draw on real life and legal transcripts to suggest that DNA evidence extracted from semen is the product of specialized, technical, and scientific processes and is therefore inherently infallible. We, as viewers, are led to believe that the objective nature of such evidence makes it perhaps the only truly reliable evidence in a case.

ANTHROPOMORPHIZED SEMEN

As discussed previously, anthropomorphism is the act of attributing human forms or qualities to entities, which are not human or singularly capable of attaining "personhood." While sperm in children's books are most commonly anthropomorphized as cheerful, smiling, determined tadpoles, *CSI* uses anthropomorphism to different effect. Sperm as evidence is most often benignly referred to as a "stain"[39] or as the "donor," even in a murder or rape investigation. In some episodes, instead of referring to sperm as an object, a vernacular of personhood is used such as "these guys" and "little soldiers," or sperm is part of a "menage d'allele" (referring to a ménage a trois because three different DNA profiles were recovered from inside a woman's body).

I would argue that sperm are anthropomorphized to create an affinity for the cells and to liken them to men. They are soldiers going to battle or sex partners engaging in fantastic encounters. These representations imply some cognition and motivation on the part of the sperm and the man. As stand-ins for actual men, many sperm depictions do not degrade the character of men; rather, they play on ideals of men as soldiers and sexual schemers—guys' guys. Representations of sperm can also be derogatory; the perpetrator is not a "real man" because he is incapable of "normal" sexual conquest.

Sperm, as little soldiers or guys, are in the service of their producers. For example, in a *CSI* episode entitled "Boom," the little soldiers are actually able to exonerate one possible perpetrator (Nick, who is also a CSI). Investigating the murder of a prostitute, Greg uses a microscope to identify biologics. He sees Nick's sperm and dubs them, "Nick's little soldiers." Catherine asks him, "When did you say this sample was frozen?" Greg answers, "About 10:15 A.M. Why?" Catherine shoots back, "These guys are all heads, no tails." Later, Catherine explains her theory to Grissom: "The sperm found in the condom was frozen at 10:15 A.M. It's all heads, no tails. It takes about seven hours for bacteria to eat away at the tails, placing the time of ejaculation at two A.M." Due to the life span of sperm and the method by which they disintegrate, Catherine is able to provide reasonable doubt that Nick was the murderer of a prostitute.

Anthropomorphism can also be used as a ploy to degrade the male character's masculinity. For example, the *CSI* episode entitled "One Hit Wonder" opens with the camera shooting through a keyhole and into a bedroom where there's a woman screaming. A man is straddled on top of her on the bed. She continues to scream, and the man runs away as the screen fades to white. During the investigation, after a frustrating experience of finding only preejaculate in the victim's hair, which Catherine reminds us "carries no DNA," Greg finds ejaculate that contains DNA outside a victim's window. He states, "The ejaculate outside the first girl's window—spank high. Good news: It does have DNA." When he says, "spank high" he uses his hand to place it a bit above waist level. And even though the sperm is able to be shot high up on the window, Greg continues, "Well, I can tell you this about him: Really low sperm count. Sample hardly had any swimmers." Nick adds, "That's probably from excessive masturbation. Guy's been outpacing his ability to produce sperm." This comment draws smirks from his coworkers as they dub Nick "Spanky."

Even though having "hardly any swimmers" in your semen could indicate excessive masturbation or simply lots of sex with a partner, the investigators in this *CSI* episode focus on the former to construct their perpetrator as a "submasculine" bad guy. The man who has nonswimming semen is not athletic and is incapable of attracting women. He is not able to be a donor, and he cannot attract a woman in whom to make a deposit. Because of his familiarity with the etiology of low sperm count, Nick may even degrade his own claims to masculinity as the quick banter reveals. Men's semen must live up to the cultural standards of hegemonic masculinity, or men and their semen are ridiculed.

SEMEN AS DECOY

In some instances, sperm are manipulated by investigators to entrap the men believed to be guilty of a crime. Decoys are used. In the *CSI* episode "Strip Strangler," the perpetrator is "planting hairs, planting semen." Where is he planting them? The woman's body is not visible, nor are her anatomical parts specified. Greg reports, "The semen recovered at this morning's homicide matches the semen taken from the bed sheets of the last two female victims." Catherine, curiously looking at the red-stained semen, says, "Freakiest semen I've seen in a while. Call me." In another scene it is called "indeterminate red stuff."' The red stuff, ketchup, was mixed into the semen found at the scene of each of the Strip Strangler's crimes, as concocted and placed by the perpetrator. Catherine ventures, "I guess we should've known, our guy was planting hairs, he was planting semen." This episode explores the way the *CSI* team must stay one step ahead of the criminals. Because knowledge about the evidentiary value of semen has been mass produced, now criminals are able to use semen to trick the investigators.

In these television shows, I would argue that what is really sought is moral certainty through the reliance on medical knowledge. The more reliable the DNA evidence is, the more certain one's moral judgment will be. The shows are akin to the lurid and morally absolute reality screaming matches on daytime TV, in that crimes of sexual violence and deviance, such as rape, incest, and sodomy, evoke intense emotional responses. In a society of increasingly cultural, ethnic, and economic diversity, television has become a convenient dispenser of simple morality. While leaked semen on TV figures prominently in morally charged messages of sexually deviant taboos, the discourse around DNA evidence helps provide a calm, rational path to the moral high ground.

Much as semen in children's books provides children with ideas about what is normal regarding reproduction, semen in television crime series reinforce these stories by constructing stories of certainty, moral reprehension, and the punitive retribution exacted from violators.

"SO, WHY DO YOU HAVE THIS
BIG SEMEN STAIN IN YOUR UNDERWEAR?"

Perhaps some of the fascination with these crime shows is because semen does not just leak during violent crimes. It can also leak during furtive, intimate moments that are secretly shared between consenting adults. The at-home infidelity testing industry has capitalized on a growing market of suspicious partners that want to collect physical evidence of infidelity. Reflecting another aspect of the "CSI effect," infidelity tests encourage laypeople to draw definitive conclusions in their temporary role as forensic investigators. The companies that benefit from this niche market prey on suspicion as a means to generate profits. These companies target male partners who are suspicious of their female partner's infidelities. As companies' advertise, an individual can either purchase an at-home kit for semen detection or send away samples of "panties, nighties, sheets, condoms, tampons" for more costly laboratory testing. According to testimonials on the website getcheckmate.com, many people make important decisions based on the outcome of these tests.[40] As someone from Tyler, Texas writes:

> As a man experiencing a tumultuous time in his marriage, I was troubled with the mixed feelings. Is it stress, a newborn child, mid-life crisis, or was there someone else involved? Not knowing is the worst of feelings. I was putting my clothes in the dirty clothes hamper and I inadvertently noticed a stain in my wife's underwear. Now I was certainly suspicious. A few days later after she was out of town again I noticed a similar stain. Now I was worried and needed a definitive answer. I searched the web and found out about checkmate. I was apprehensive as you would expect but I gave it a try. I received the kit promptly and discretely and tested both garments against a known semen sample. To my surprise and relief the 2 tests were negative, and the known sample showed positive in about 4 seconds! My marriage is certainly no stronger but at least the worries of infidelity won't com-

plicate trying to fix it or end it. Truly a great product and a good value if you think about what it really does.[41]

One company, genuServe.com, offers home fidelity kits and laboratory services with the following price tags. To determine whether a stain or fluid is semen with or without sperm cells, in June 2006, prices range from $195 to $995, depending on how quickly you want the results. To compare one evidence sample to one suspect sample costs $1,200. DNA extraction tests semen contained in condoms, jars, plastic bottles, or other sterile containers and runs $300. Additionally, dnatestingcentre.com provides condom matching, which determines whether cells outside of the condom match a DNA sample you provide, to see whose body the condom has been inserted into. However, the website notes that there is only a 50 percent chance of DNA being extracted from the outside of the condom. Regardless of the ability to achieve results, the service costs $580. So even using a condom to contain the "evidence" may not prevent the lay sleuth from gathering evidence.

At sementest.com, ForenseX Laboratory Corp., an Arizona-based company urges, "Send us your dirty panties." Another website, infidelity.com, boasts to be "The # 1 Source for Semen Stain Detection Tests." An article from a London-based website states that in 2001 Checkmate sold 1,000 kits a month, 85 percent of their clients were men, nearly half of their customers have been married 15 years or more, and 40 percent were over 40 years old.[42] This kit is primarily aimed at testing "flowback"—that is, semen that drains into undergarments for up to 72 hours after intercourse. The test is specially formulated to detect certain enzymes produced by the male prostate gland, which is found in semen. The cost of at-home testing, $69.00 for testing 10 articles, contrasted to hiring a private investigator at about $1,000 minimum fee, is marketed as one of the product's major benefits. The ad also suggests that women who are cheating on their partners are usually in a rush and don't clean up very thoroughly, possibly leaving traces of semen on different parts of the inside of their clothing.

The sales pitches and slogans of these products are sensational. A cartoon on the website infidelitykit.com illustrates a woman with a surprised look on her face saying, "I don't know how that semen got in my underwear!" The sites are straightforward in their claims and appeals:

Just imagine how many men who were doing laundry when they inadvertently came across a stain, they had no real way to identify.[43]

Checkmate replaces Dog as man's best friend.[44]

Will give you scientific truth about the infidelity or fidelity of your mate.[45]

Don't be made a fool of by a cheating wife or a cheating wife's lover. Stop hurting and know the scientific truth.[46]

She brings the evidence home to you without even knowing it.[47]

Make an informed decision.[48]

Remember the Clinton Rule, check all clothing. Cheating is cheating.[49]

Did you know that semen, blood and saliva can be detected on clothing or bedding and that DNA technology can say who those stains came from or didn't come from?[50]

What type of man is being constructed in these statements? Clearly, these sites attempt to exploit men's insecurity, suspicion, and doubt regarding their partner's fidelity and their own ability to retain and satisfy that partner. Men who might use these sites may not be able to afford a private detective, or they cannot afford to lose in a "messy" divorce. But there is also an obvious appeal to traditionally masculine qualities such as scientific rationality and the desire for hard proof. With a direct, no-nonsense style, these statements command men to take control of their situation.

While most of the marketing is targeted primarily to a male consumer, there are also testing services available for women who are suspicious of their male partners. These sites claim that men secrete semen up to two hours after intercourse or oral sex; consequently, semen will be in their underwear. There are no catchy headings on the webpages about a woman's best friend. Women are untrustworthy, but that is only because there are other men and other sperm out there that want access to these women. Infidelity kits allow for the creative and potentially deceitful manipulation of semen. For example, there is nothing preventing someone in the midst of a messy divorce case from getting hold of a woman's panties, having a male friend stain them, and then sending them in for testing.

The currently available technology employed by fidelity kits relies exclusively on the presence of semen. The authority to definitively answer questions of infidelity rests with semen. While women can be either suspected of infidelity or removed from suspicion, the only time a woman can get definitive results from this type of testing is if her partner is involved in homosexual activity. The heterosexual male is in the most advantageous position. To date, there are no definitive biological tests for women to employ to determine if their male partners are participating in sex with other women.

SNEAKY AND LEAKY

Throughout the past 300 years, semen has emerged as one of the most important totems. Semen is imbued with extremely intense social meanings, including birth, death, disease, virility, sex, violence, love, hatred, and genetic heritage. Semen comes from the male body; it is constantly produced throughout the lifespan of the man, and it is ejaculated, intentionally and accidentally. It is strong and tenacious. Semen can endure in vaginas and on fabrics. While semen is collectible, it is not easy for the ejaculator to catch unless there are prior arrangements made to entrap it. Therefore, it can be messy and unpredictable, often leaving recalcitrant track marks for others to find. People who are the recipients of semen have a difficult time getting rid of it; and when it is spilled, semen leaves an evidentiary trail that leads to one specific man. By establishing methods of seminal detection, professional and lay forensic practitioners are now able to locate semen, describe the type of sex men and women are performing (normal or perverted), and, ultimately, substantiate an act of intercourse.

Sperm is a sneaky and leaky silent witness. Once coveted and assumed dangerous because of its ability to impregnate, through biotechnological innovation semen has become the equivalent of mobile identifiers (swimming mini-mes). A man can be identified and defined by the actions of his sperm. With both the means and the authority, the state now can codify sperm cells, making sperm and the individual men who produce it inherently knowable and identifiable. The state can offer us mechanisms to make us feel safer through the codification and translation of the code, but there are trade-offs, especially the loss of privacy through criminal profiling using a public database of "dangerous" men that is subject to bias in its construction and abuse in its deployment. As Dorothy Nelkin and Lori Andrews point out, using CODIS to slowly chip away at citizen privacy and civil liberties was strategic:

State statutes vary. Most statutes initially required that saliva and blood samples be obtained from sex offenders on their release from prison, or as a condition of probation or parole. Statistically, sex offenders do have a high rate of recidivism. Strategically, selecting a group with such a negative public image for mandatory DNA testing was unlikely to provoke objections. . . . In Virginia, those convicted of mail fraud must also store samples. . . . In Wisconsin, if a judge determines that a crime "might have escalated to a sex crime" he can require registration. At least seven states test misdemeanants.[51]

Through their sperm, many men are databased into the FBI's CODIS system. CODIS is technically sophisticated and can officially structure masculinities in a hierarchical schema. "Bad" men—or more appropriately stated, poor, disenfranchised, low-status men—have little ability to avoid being placed in a database that can readily trace their identities. CODIS therefore creates a surveillance system that enhances bureaucratic power and works in conjunction with stratification systems to keep some men in control while keeping others under control. In the case of sexual assault crimes, seminal evidence becomes the conduit by which there is justification to corral men (who do not have the resources to avoid the detention). Through seminal evidence in pretext arrests, many men, not guilty of the crime, have been added to the ranks of CODIS.

Just as women have been constructed as sexually undependable and vulnerable, men are now becoming scientifically constructed as sexually suspect—that is, cultural beliefs about certain men as sexually unreliable and suspect are being scientifically and medically legitimated. Furthermore, men are being constructed as driven and defined by their sexuality and male bodies. Similar to traditional notions of female bodies, men's motives and essential "nature" are now recognizable by their bodily fluids.

The development of DNA analysis has created another social arena in which moral stories about specific men and women can be told. Semen is represented repeatedly as a reflection of men's morality. Stained sheets are taken as seminal evidence that a man has spilled his seed. He could not control himself and stay in line with societal norms; he is uncivilized. Semen is at once signified and signifier—it is represented by social constructs that imbue it with meaning (signified), and it represents the social construction of its producer, man (signifier). My analysis of sperm as evidence, within the scientific historical record, the entertainment industry, and the at-home testing marketplace, illustrates how sperm has become an integral component in the processes of adjudication. Perhaps the moral certainty of DNA comes not just from getting the right perp but from a pervasive reproduction of gender, sexuality, and racial ideologies. We watch these shows and root for the "good guys" to avenge the "passive victims" (i.e., women) by getting the "bad guys." Sperm as DNA samples are the tools used to reproduce these ideologies and hierarchies. Sperm are us, in a strange way; we see what we want to see and hear the stories we want to hear about men and women. Even the jurors who want lots of evidence because they've seen it on TV want to be entertained, and they want their preconceived notions about the world reproduced.

Driven by advances in DNA testing and forensic technologies, the investigation and prosecution of violent crimes now rely primarily on physical evidence rather than on testimony, narrative, and interrogation. Now a process of scientific rationalization, sleuthing is no longer an art or an interpretive experience; rather, it exemplifies a quest for certainty, where the presence of semen or other DNA-laden evidence has become a basis for this certainty. In this process, we are witnessing the conflation of inference and deduction. Investigations are no longer reliant on the interrogation of a person but on the bodily by-product of that person (blood, hair, cells, sperm, DNA). Sperm, as a silent, certain witness, is now becoming the only witness as well.

Surveillance of human bodies is becoming more insidious and more difficult to avoid. The DNA Act of 2000 enabled authorities to force extraction of samples from state-mandated qualifying offenses. For example, in New York State, DNA identification information must be provided by anyone convicted and sentenced in crimes, including criminal tampering, tampering with a consumer product, patronizing a prostitute, falsely reporting an incident, placing a false bomb or hazardous substance, and unlawful wearing of a body vest.[52] Governor George Pataki praised his own legislation: "Today, because of the tough, new crime legislation we've passed, New York is the safest large state in the country. By putting in place new initiatives, like an expanded DNA databank, we can achieve our ambitious goal of making New York the safest of any state in America."[53] And the Bush administration's $1 billion initiative on Advancing Justice through DNA technology all but ensures that the amplification of surveillance of human bodies and their evidentiary trails will increase in the future.

7

The Future of Sperm

Sperm counts as never before. Our culture is fascinated by sperm. The substance is more visible, more discussed, and more researched than in previous centuries. But while knowledge about and access to sperm have grown, the substance itself has become more complicated. This is partly because as our fascination with sperm grows, so do social movements that enable more democratic participation in scientific research, forensic investigation, and sperm banking. As I try to show throughout this book, sperm is at the same time more interesting, complicated, and specialized, and yet more accessible, programmable, deployable, and predictable than ever before.

What are the meanings that have accrued about semen? Depending on the circumstances of ejaculation, it can be desired or reviled. In order to be useful for fertility, it must be the right shape, the right speed, and in the right quantity. Reproductive scientists and zoologists have defined sperm as homunculi, eels, kamikaze fighters, and invaders. Semen banks have invented technosemen as a new and improved commodity for sale. The fatherhood rights movement advocates that semen is a man's property deserving legislative protection; this belies the fear that making semen more accessible threatens traditional notions of fatherhood. Writers and illustrators of children's books depict sperm as friendly competitors and romancers following through on cross-species evolutionary drives or God's plan. Forensic scientists, at-home sleuths, and "real-life" crime stories have established seminal stains as the gold standard of evidence and as the ultimate link to identity. Sex workers attempt to contain it as "hazardous waste material," while pornographers fetishize the money shot with lights, camera, and action.

Sperm's meaning thus circulates around its discovery, production, and representation. Although the varying social worlds in which these meanings are created are vast in their composition of distinct resources, their varying degrees of legitimacy and their use of particular devices of inscription for different understandings of semen, they each rely on constructing an expertise about semen and an understanding of a potential user's relationship with that semen.[1] In the end, each of these social worlds—the pornographic, the scientific, and so on—develops and projects their own theories and attitudes about men, semen, health, and disease.

The proliferation of new uses and access to sperm has the potential to alter social structures in dramatic and liberating ways. For example, technical innovation of scientific tools and transformations in our understanding of gender and sexuality have given lesbians and single women new access to sperm through semen banks. This access to sperm for reproductive purposes has real effects and provides new possibilities of liberation, particularly for single women and gays and lesbians. In this case, sperm is a tool that can deconstruct traditional gender relations and allow new types of families to emerge. That said, the new practices that sperm allows still have not produced full-scale social changes because many of the people involved in these procedures still control the meaning of sperm in fairly conservative ways. By narrowly controlling the meanings of sperm as evidence of male dominance or heterosexuality—as most sperm banks, children's books, and forensic analyses do—the potentially threatening or liberating (depending on your point of view) material possibilities of sperm are limited.

SEMEN AS MEN AS SEMEN

Throughout this book, I provide examples of how the separation between semen/sperm and men/boys is diffuse. Because semen comes exclusively from male bodies and because men have been so central in the scientific discovery of semen and the subsequent proliferation of seminal enterprises (such as pornography, forensics, and fatherhood rights), it seems to me that men are clearly invested in the representations of semen as inherently linked to their sense of selfhood. In other words, men (as well as women) have represented semen through ideas about masculinity as a way of mirroring back some measure of the man. There has been a long history of seepage between the represented and the representation. The more masculine the man, the more manly his semen, and vice versa.

What I have tried to demonstrate throughout the book is how the representations of sperm become a direct or an indirect proxy (or both) for the characteristics of the producer, the man. However, we've seen that sperm are not just the embodiment of men; at times, men also become endowed with the characteristics of their sperm. At a crime scene where seminal stains may implicate a specific man, these sperm cells are direct proxies for men. Sperm are also indirect proxies for men where men's social or physical characteristics are associated with scientific attributes of their sperm such as size, speed, count, velocity, and volume. For example, several of my male friends who have had semen analysis have assured me in a joking yet cocky way that their counts were high. The implication is that if you have a high sperm count, then you are a real man.

Men are also seen as proxies for their sperm. For example, if a sperm donor is healthy, the sperm is assumed to be healthy. If the man is a sexual powerhouse, his ejaculate will be voluminous and forceful. In this bidirectional association, sperm can indicate the health or degree of masculinity of the man, and the man can indicate the health or degree of masculinity of the sperm.

And just like men, through education, exercise, diet, steroids, and cosmetic surgery, semen can be enhanced and improved. The hierarchies of masculinity are ever more specific. In other words, men are measured against one another based on increasingly detailed systems of evaluation. The understanding of seminal fluid, its ability to be measured in increasingly specific ways, provides new means to explore its worth. New rankings continually replace the old.

Seminal industries, including semen banking and pornography, participate in creating hegemonic and hierarchical constructions of men, whereby certain social and physiological characteristics are perceived to be more desirable than others. Tall men, smart men, professionally successful men, healthy men, young men, men with large penises and long-lasting erections—all these aspects are advertised to "move" the inventory (the semen, the books, the videos). Men are ranked in terms of popularly consumed notions about semen, with significant social implications. When semen and sperm are assigned qualities such as "healthy," "virile," "sexy," "abundant," or "powerful," some men rise up, while other men (and their semen) are marginalized and disempowered. As a result, based on how their sperm is counted, some men are seen as more powerful, desirable, and masculine, and others are seen as disempowered, undesirable, and emasculated.

But in order for a man to participate in certain seminal industries, his semen must be evaluated and screened. In the case of semen banks, it is tested, manipulated, and even improved. Indeed, the best semen is not natural; it is processed and refined through technology, giving us what I call technosemen. In the semen banking industry, semen is extracted from the male body, and powerful meanings are assigned to the final product. These meanings are based on the characteristics of the donor, as well as on the technical expertise of semen bank owner and operators. Semen banks design and produce technosemen as a way to market sperm as safe, fertile, and even desirable. Through the scientific rationality of medical screening and the emotional appeal of donor catalogues, donor sperm is represented as both embodying and improving upon the man who produced it. In other words, semen banks mitigate the risks that women (and possibly their male partners) might fear by marketing their technologically enhanced semen. In semen banks' donor catalogues, as in children's books, sperm is anthropomorphized to reestablish and amplify the relationship of the semen to its producer. These anthropomorphized images of semen are used to create semen as asexual, safe, and friendly.

But semen, and by proxy the men who produce it, can also be cast as unhealthy, weak, and undesirable. Sex workers have created innovative practices to manage and control semen to avoid exposure to AIDS and other sexually transmitted diseases. Men and their bodily fluids are perceived by sex workers as a risk to be contained. The increasing prevalence of male infertility has spawned an entire lexicon to describe substandard sperm. More than objective, scientific metrics about fertility, motility, sperm count, and morphology also measure men and their masculinity.

With increasing reliance on DNA testing to help identify suspects, federal, state, and local law enforcement agencies have embraced systems such as the FBI's CODIS database. CODIS enables investigators to quickly "round up the usual suspects," but when the database is being populated with semen samples from pretext arrests, innocent lower-status men become suspects, too. As DNA testing technology has become more affordable and accessible, its application to semen and sperm cells has gone mainstream. From popular crime shows on television to do-it-yourself infidelity test kits, DNA testing of sperm cells leads one to the truth with scientific certainty.

DNA testing of semen usually is performed to identify perpetrators of specific violent crimes that involve sexual activity. Similar testing of female sexual fluids is neither commonplace nor pursued as vigorously. As a result, semen analysis provides an additional means of social control over the actions of men, but not of women. Thus semen is defined, managed, and represented as evidentiary for the protection of women from men. The rise of at-home testing is marketed to men suspicious of other men. Semen as evidence also has the potential to protect men from sexual violence from other men, but not much is heard about this taboo subject. Thus, the social situations in which semen analyses are performed seem to be defined by hegemonically masculine notions of sex and crime; as with Clinton and Bryant, the semen must have gotten where it did by the accuser's wrongdoing. In these cases, seminal evidence might be a proud display of prowess, enhancing myth-making and popularity. But the threat of sperm cells also has emerged as a way to disable certain men from full participation in civil society; after all, their male cells might be codified within FBI databases.

Reactions to these contemporary constructions of sperm and semen can be seen in various social worlds. The fetishization of semen in pornography, from the traditional "money shot" to the newer "semen shots," is one example. In these movies, the taboo consumption of semen is eroticized and thereby transformed from potentially unhealthy to sexy and desirable. Another example is fathers' rights movements, which, I argue, are reacting to a large extent to developments in the semen banking industry and other new reproductive technologies such as ICSI, surrogacy, and IVF. With the increasing prevalence of sperm bank babies and alternate family structures, traditional notions of fatherhood and paternity are in flux.

Semen binds social groups together by giving them common frames of reference as well as objects of contention; sperm is an object of interaction around which social relations are determined. As my analyses show, currently there are a variety of industries in which sperm's fluidity of meanings congeal with clear social implications for men and masculinity. In the end, what matters more is not whether or not the meaning of sperm is fluid, but under what conditions this fluidity of meanings solidifies into certain forms of social life and then understanding their social implications.

SPERM IN THE FUTURE

Understanding semen in contemporary cultures means we must also account for the inherent instability of masculinity. Due to extreme shifts in cultural values, biotechnological innovation, and economic and geopolitical instability, traditional beliefs and representations of masculinity are now threatened. The preexisting ideal types of men and prevailing expressions of a rugged masculinity are being rendered obsolete or impossible to achieve—male breadwinner, father, protector, warrior. During these times of intense reorganization of male power, particularly experienced in the last 25 years, there is a battle for agency between men and their sperm. Semen does not merely represent men; it has taken on a life of its own. Men, as supremely rational beings, are taken over by their sperm. Sperm drive men to masturbate, compete, reproduce, ejaculate, infect, and incriminate themselves. Perhaps, as some industries would have it, men are ultimately controlled by their sperm (instead of their penises). As a result, many sites of seminal representation illustrate how men have been commandeered by their sperm.

Sperm cells, similar to the oft-cited sway of testosterone and penises, are portrayed as powerful forces, and men cannot be wholly responsible for the actions of their sperm or of how their sperm might make them act. But men, unlike women, cannot be entirely relegated to being driven by physical limitations of cells, hormones, or body parts. So there are continuous examples of how men can wrest control of the animalistic agency of sperm through rational and technological ingenuity. In this battle for control, men simultaneously represent their sperm as all-powerful (particularly when a real man cannot be there to represent himself, as in the case of children's books or reproductive science) but then have to rein in their sperm so as not to be dominated by it.

As shown throughout this book, the social purpose of semen has been produced and recast over several centuries. But what are today's possible consequences, outcomes, and trajectories of the tremendous social changes in men's lives relative to their social power? Permit me to prognosticate. If environmental trends continue, polluting the natural resource of male bodies, there could be a massive decline in the availability of sperm. Male factor infertility trends could continue in a downward spiral, leading to a reliance on banked sperm. Prices of banked sperm could skyrocket, and a black market of vials of semen would emerge, creating the need for governmental intervention to police the illegal sperm industry. Due to current market forces, legitimate semen banks maintain a fairly homogenous stock. After a couple of generations, we could be facing a race/diversity crisis, as well as a cost-access concern, as only those who can afford sperm will be able to reproduce.

And how might fathers remake their identity without sperm? One outcome would be a more expansive notion of fatherhood, not reliant on a known genetic connection with offspring. Alternatively, "real" dads could become elite men. Some men might even fake being "real" dads, perhaps creating even more secrets about how reproduction occurs.[2] In this scenario, new grades of fatherhood might emerge where it could be considered low-tech or backward to have conceived a child with fresh embodied semen. Children's books would recast the heroes of the reproductive fairy tale: "Because he loved you and Mommy so much, Daddy made a lot of money and looked at every catalogue to search for the perfect sperm cell. And we picked out the very best sperm to make you. We had to wait in a very long line, but Daddy gave the sperm bank director extra money because you were so wanted." Or perhaps in line with the Christian children's books: "It made God so happy that we wanted to have you, and He led us to the chosen sperm bank. It's all part of God's plan."

In pornography, even though there is still ejaculate, the substance might be viewed differently without sperm inside. Might it come to pass that the value of sperm would become so great that it couldn't be "wasted" on women? Imagine hearing men say, "I can make more selling my sperm at the bank than I can being a porn star." What would the new money shot be? Perhaps alternative fetishes and fluids would come to the fore, such as female ejaculation.

For investigators and prosecutors reliant on DNA forensics, increasing male infertility would mean the loss of a significant pool of evidence. The presence of semen at a crime scene might indicate the nature of the crime, but it would no longer tell us anything about the perpetrator's identity. Presuming a world with nearly universal male infertility, consider the status of the rare male who can still produce sperm. He might be a king, a porn star, a gold mine, or a medical oddity. Or he may be just a regular guy as new notions of masculinity emerge. Semen and sperm are central to conceptions of men's reproductive agency, sexual power, and their identity as fathers. As the links between sperm and men are severed in many ways, what it means to count as a man may have nothing to do with sperm, and vice versa.

Methods Appendix

Becoming a Sperm Researcher

As a researcher trained in the sociological traditions of grounded theory, feminist interpretive inquiry, and qualitative methods, I want to detail the specifics of the research process I undertook before writing this book. This methods appendix provides background information about my studies of sperm—specifically, why I chose to study it, what sources of data I used, and how I went about gathering and interpreting that data. Like many before me, I am interested in the traffic between scientific and popular worlds, especially through interpreting cases that demonstrate a cross-fertilization of science and culture whereby the two are inextricably linked. Meanings about semen accrue through practices and uses, and these meanings bleed into one another. Many different social institutions (science and medicine, the family, the criminal justice system) participate in describing and thus making sperm meaningful as a social object. These institutions do not exist within a vacuum, and as a sociologist, I work to contextualize these industries. They are all part of a contemporary moment in which men's power and status are being questioned and reconfigured (as well as being reproduced and maintained). Interpreting different social worlds' portrayals of sperm, I work to reveal the rules by which sperm becomes "good" and "bad," "productive" and "destructive." In so doing, I hope to elevate the field of gender and sexuality studies by extrapolating from semen how contemporary Western men are depicted.

I began this research project in 1990 and I still consider it a work in progress. It may seem paradoxical to some that as a lesbian mother of two daughters and a feminist sociologist, I could find sustained interest in human sperm. At this point, there are limited opportunities in my personal life that put me in direct contact with sperm—I don't produce it, and neither do any of my immediate family members. Over 10 years ago, I had to use sperm to get pregnant. Despite the meticulous attention I paid to semen then (its color, odor, viscosity, amount), it doesn't really enter my consciousness now when I think about my daughters. Still, my professional life has been dominated by understanding, describing, and theorizing this substance. I find the cultural preoccupation with this male body fluid fascinating. Perhaps a Freudian analyst could see this fascination as a form of envy or desire for what I lack. However, I see this fascination with semen and sperm as an entry point to further my own intellectual and political interests in men, masculinity, and processes of reifying male domination. For me, the process of following semen as it flows through male bodies, discharges from the penis, and circulates through the culture has taken me to some quite unexpected places.

Drawing on the fields of science and technology studies, medical sociology, and social studies of gender and sexuality, this project is an investigation into how semen occupies the spaces created when these fields overlap. Although this book is neither exhaustive nor representative of the entire realm of semen and spermatic representations, I studied a range of sources, including scientific and historical documents of biomedical discovery, texts about the U.S. fatherhood rights movement, and narrative evidence of the traffic between biological accounts of sperm and social accounts of men (through weblogs, popular text, etc.) Combined with my own ethnographic experiences in the semen banking industry, I also analyzed sperm bank promotional materials.

1990–1996

My experiences with sperm data sources began with my tenure at the Sperm Bank of California. As a board member of TSBC, I did not collect data or formally interview anyone for six years. But I was immersed in a world where I developed a fluency in how sperm is both used and constructed in relation to donor insemination. During this time, sperm became known to me as inventory that was fragile and costly to maintain. It was also a commodity to be stylized and marketed. "Tall sperm" went quickly, for example, so the sperm bank considered shorter men (under 5 feet 6 inches) to be less desirable as donors. TSBC's low-cost ad campaign in male bathrooms at the University of California at Berkeley stated, "Get Paid for What You're Already Doing." But not all sperm (or donors) were created equal. The demand for sperm from certain types of men (and lack of demand for others) revealed clearly that certain donor characteristics (such as height) were perceived as more desirable to TSBC customers.

Despite knowing I could not collect data while I was working at the sperm bank, I did find another way to obtain data: donor catalogues. Prior to widespread use of the internet as a means to advertise donor semen, it was common practice for semen banks to publish printed donor catalogues. Finding an accurate list of the entire sperm donor population was impossible, however, because semen banks were (and still are) not regulated by any federal agency. Instead, the industry is self-regulated by the American Association of Tissue Banks (AATB), a member-based group. Using the 1997/1998 AATB list of accredited tissue and semen banks, I wrote to the entire list of 46 sperm banks requesting their donor catalogues. Thirty-five banks responded with donor catalogues; many included letters from the executive director or president of the bank addressed to "Mrs. Moore," mentioning a nonexistent husband and requesting that I send a photograph of him for donor matching. Using donor catalogues as data, I coded the materials and created dimensions of the codes to write analytic memos.

During this fieldwork, sperm emerged as a significant social object for my informants. This research included over five years of field work conducting 27 semi-structured interviews with 19 self-identified sex workers. Conducting this research in the San Francisco Bay Area enabled me access to a diverse community of research subjects and colleagues. San Francisco, rich in racial, ethnic, and sexual diversity, and home to a large gay and lesbian community, provides fertile ground for both collecting data and interpreting issues in human sexuality. The age, clientele, price ranges, and work sites enable these sex workers to negotiate greater power and control in the sex work situation.

My pilot work of interviewing sex workers, in 1992–1993, focused on interpretations of their narratives about body image and emotional work during their sexual work practices. These first ventures into the world of the sex industry were scary, exciting, awkward, informative, and provocative. I felt as if I had established links with a particular group of people and wanted very much to convey their stories through my research. Aided by a generous, patient, and clever key informant, Quincy, with whom I had been politically active in several health and sexuality based organizations and movements, I established contact with 30 sex workers during 1994–1996. These sex workers were all over 18 with a median age in their late 30s. The major requirement for inclusion in my interview sample was the sex worker's self-acknowledged consensual engagement in sexual activities that involved controlling the exchange of body fluids. These sex workers, working on a freelance and relatively autonomous basis, are career sex workers and are not drug dependent. Most are actively involved in community-based organizations for health education, sex worker rights, and feminist advocacy.

Quincy's connections and reputation tremendously assisted my entry into the sex work community. Her introductions afforded me the possibility and confidence to build rapport within a very specific, and in some ways closed and protected, community. In her unacknowledged but carefully assumed role as gatekeeper, Quincy met with me to evaluate my interview questions, offering suggestions about the interview structure and linguistic cues to help me become an insider. For example, during this meeting, I received a crash course in "sex work 101" with a definition list of terms like "in-call," "out-call," "doubles," and "a half and half." An in-call is doing sexual sessions at the worker's location. An out-call is doing sexual sessions at an external site, generally the client's home or business. Doubles is doing sexual sessions with two workers. A half and half is performing oral sex on a man to the point of ejaculation and then starting and completing sexual intercourse (usually penis-vagina penetration). I have written about the transformations of these sex workers' professional selves through practicing a sexual trade in the time of AIDS/HIV to become competent experts of sperm control.[1] I have also analyzed their work practices to discuss the configuration of users to latex devices such as male and female condoms, dental dams, and finger cots, and the practical, symbolic, and material innovation of such devices.

1997–2001

As I explain in the introduction to this volume, my own relationship to sperm spans the personal and the professional. As a pregnant woman and then mother, my interest in semen shifted because I felt a responsibility to explain to my daughters the legitimacy of their origin stories. An initial review of children's facts-of-life books provided little, if any, exploration of alternative families, but plenty of interesting material on sperm. I knew it would be very difficult to gain access to a sample of young readers under 12 to further investigate how these books might be understood and consumed by their target audience. Indeed, since academic researchers must get Committee on Human Subjects Research approval from their college's Institutional Review Board, it is likely that many researchers (including this one) would get derailed in endless bureaucracy and revisions of forms.[2]

I wanted to replicate those nostalgic and warm memories of my own introduction to reproduction on the couch with my mother. But as I surveyed the multiple cultural, social, economic, and material contexts of sperm representation in children's books, I was disappointed. Thumbing through these facts-of-life books and imagining reading them to my daughters was both exciting and a bit terrifying. The presumption of heterosexuality was ubiquitous, and the renderings of sperm as heroic were relentless. Through a more detailed comparison of two types of books, I found that secular and Christian children's books differ in their approach to assigning reproductive agency. For the purposes of this study, 27 children's books were analyzed. The books chosen were based on the following criteria: written in the English language, representation of sperm through narrative or visual images, text based, an intended audience of children aged 4–12.

This was certainly not an exhaustive or representative study of all children's books on human reproduction. However, I did work to incorporate a range of variation based on multiple dimensions. For example, the publication dates spanned between 1952 and 2001. I also varied the gender of author: 9 were men, 16 were women, and 3 were co-authored by a male/female team. The types of illustrations were different: 3 were photographic, 15 were cartoon animation, 5 were painted, and 5 were pen and ink drawing. The stated ideology of the books were from two realms: 8 were religious, specifically Christian, and 20 were secular books. Each book was read and analyzed by a single coder, myself. All the books, sperm representations, and narratives about sperm were assigned categories (e.g., scientific, humorous, religious), and dimensions were then assigned (e.g., anthropomorphized, nonhuman and speaking, nonspeaking, personhood). Analytic memos were written to explore these categories and dimensions. To check coder reliability, a second analyst, a colleague and previous collaborator trained in grounded theory, Matthew Schmidt, recoded the books.

For the purposes of this volume, I have asked the following questions about children's facts-of-life books: What are the contexts in which sperm may be represented in children's books? What are some of the underlying ideologies that can be extrapolated from these contexts and representations? How do children's books represent the state-of-the-art scientific innovations in sperm science? In other words, if science constructs a "truth" of sperm to be mostly polymorphic, often nonmotile, and sometimes dwindling, are children's books incorporating these differences in their text? Are assisted reproductive technologies considered as valid ways to become pregnant? Are deformed or slow sperm represented at all? How? Are there "gay sperm" or other nonnormative, renegade sperm represented in children's books? How gendered are textual and visual narratives of sperm? Are there portrayals of male bonding or bullying in sperm representations?

2001–2006

While children's books may make a passing reference to DNA, or more commonly to heredity, in their contents, understanding sperm as containing DNA led me to another aspect of sperm use. DNA forensics both incriminates and exonerates men often based on their leaky semen. In order to more fully investigate the connections between sperm, men, and crime, I reviewed forensics and criminology textbooks to grasp the history and principles of the field. Always impressed (if not a bit in disbelief) by network television's ability to carry a large number of shows about crime, and particularly those with violent crimes against women, I started to watch shows differently. Transcripts from televisions shows (three years of *Crime Scene Investigation,* two years of *Law and Order,* two years of *NYPD Blue*) were collected, coded, and analyzed for their references to semen and sperm.

DNA forensics and television dramatizations of real life events are brought together in popular crime shows that feature the investigation of violent sex crimes, with the focus on forensic evidence. Sperm and semen, as evidence, are unlike other body fluids. Semen leaks into other bodies, male and female. It is recovered from inside of others' mouths, vaginas, and rectums. It is charged with sexual aggression, it is understood as mobile and agentic, and it is personified as a violator. There is an entire genre of entertainment that implicates seminal fluid. This mainstreaming of DNA technology through crime shows and movies has helped popularize an industry of at-home personal investigation services. Advertised on the internet, there are various at-home kits and services available for DNA sleuthing of partners and family members. After visiting over 200 websites, I chose 11 for more detailed analysis. These sites advertise at-home infidelity testing services and kits that were analyzed between September 2, 2003, and November 21, 2003. An "infidelity kits" Google search completed on September 2, 2003, listed over 2,700 sites, and of these hits at least one in 10 led to Checkmate— the most popular maker of infidelity kits.

Pornography is another social world I chose to investigate in order to more fully understand the dimensions of sperm and semen. I have watched approximately 50 hours of pornographic films and collected excerpts of descriptions of films from *Adult Video News (AVN)*, the trade paper of the porn profession. Based on this research, I think there is possibly nothing less sexy to me than pornography that glorifies semen. Literally thousands of shots of penises cumming and countless men and women bathing, drinking, writhing in semen became quickly routine. The seemingly ubiquitous image of an ejaculating penis, the money shot, became another source of data about sperm.

GROUNDING SPERM

This book is the result of my quest to create a formal grounded theory of how semen is constructed in our social worlds. Grounded theory is a deductive process, whereby analysts incorporate as much data as possible in order for the formative theories to be used as deductive tools. Through the writing and rewriting of analytic memos, grounded theory ultimately aims to incorporate the range of human experiences in its articulation and execution. According to Anselm Strauss, a key developer of grounded theory, it is through one's immersion in the data that these comparisons become the "stepping stones" for formal theories of patterns of action and interaction between and among various types of data.[3] A grounded theory analysis works to (1) generate concepts and build conceptual understandings through writing analytic memos, (2) explore and represent the range of variation of data and interpretations, and (3) use the constant comparative method to contrast like industries and basic social processes.

This book is the culmination of my quest to produce knowledge about semen and sperm in particular. A limitation of my work is that I do not have data on "what sperm means to men." Undoubtedly, this study would be fascinating, but it is outside the scope of my project. The social process of knowledge production exists within many contexts of personal and professional relationships. To explore and analyze these complex relationships, I have employed what I would call a triangulated research method. This method uses multiple data sources, asks a variety of questions, and amasses diverse perspectives. It allows for a keen, self-reflexive stance to examine the complex phenomena that produce knowledge about semen and sperm. It is only through triangulating the multiple data sources and witnessing their interaction that I am able to provide a well-rounded, theoretically robust, and creative analysis of the social origins of this body fluid.

By triangulating data sources about sperm representations over the past 10 years (scientific texts, health and social policy recommendations, children's books, popular accounts, and semen banking practices and promotional materials), I have been able to establish various points of comparison to explore multiple concepts about sperm in different environments. As stated, "Theory evolves during actual research, and it does this through continuous interplay between analysis and data collection."[4]

My methodology combines grounded theory techniques with content and discourse analysis as a way to develop theoretically rich explanations and interpretations of semen.[5] In this fashion, I am able to track the frequency of certain terms and representations, as well as the interpretative meaning and significance of these images. Similar to other qualitative research, content analysis can be exploratory and descriptive, enabling limited insight into why significant relationships or trends occur. The aim is not toward standardization of facts into scientific units but, rather, an appreciation and play with the range of variation of a particular phenomenon. Outliers, representations that do not fall neatly into the collection of the most common themes and concepts, are useful because they enable me to capture this range of variation and dimensions of the concepts. I interrogated dimensions such as the description of sperm or semen, the frequency of references to sperm, the verbs used to animate sperm, and images of sperm.

Coding, a process of going through transcripts and data sources and assigning themes to units of text, enables connections to be made between disparate sources of information. These codes are then dimen-sionalized; or as Strauss and Corbin state, codes are broken down into "location[s] of properties along a continuum."[6] So, for example, if the code was healthy sperm, the continuum would be healthy sperm on one end and unhealthy sperm on the other end. I would then look for meanings and examples of when sperm banks were trying to define healthy sperm and when they were defining unhealthy sperm. By es-tablishing the continuum, researchers can move away from simple di-chotomies and see how the relative health of sperm affects other rela-tionships. The reading of healthy sperm is then nuanced and seen as in-creasing with more manipulation by the sperm bank—there is always something more that can be done to sperm to make it better (more healthy).

I established codes according to frequency, extent, intensity, and duration. For example, one very significant code for sperm was human agency. Data from children's books were evaluated for placement on the continuum—possessing human agency to having no human agency. In vivo codes, or codes developed from informants' own words, became useful in organizing my data. For example, "sperm swim" and "little soldiers" were two in vivo codes I employed throughout coding operations.

During axial coding, the more interpretive level of coding, I inter-rogated my data to understand the conditions, contexts, strategies, and consequences of each code. I developed more specific axial coding aimed at creating properties of each code. Taking human agency as the example, I started using aspects of humanity such as consciousness, purposeful activity, morality, emotional reaction, sense of humor, and logic. Theoretical sampling, "checking on the emerging conceptual framework," involves purposefully looking at existing data for these themes and attending to these themes in the remaining interviews.[7]

Triangulation, "using multiple observers, methods, interpretive points of view and levels and forms of empirical materials in the con-struction of interpretations," adds to the adequacy of the data.[8] Sociol-ogist Norman Denzin's four categories of triangulation have served as my guide. First, data is triangulated by "search(ing) for as many data sources as possible that bear upon the events under analysis."[9] These data sources include theoretical and substantive literatures, in-depth, semi-structured interviews with sex workers and health care profes-sionals, ethnographic observations of work environments, children's books, popular television programs and historical research. Second, investigator triangulation (the use of multiple observers to increase the depth in interpretation) has been established by working with students throughout the past 10 years, working closely with colleagues, and respondent validation. Third, theoretical triangulation, exploration of the "possible interpretations in a given area," is enhanced by my use of theories of feminism, symbolic interactionism, social and cultural studies of the body, science and technology, and sex, sexuality, and gender.[10] Finally, methodological triangulation has been achieved through using grounded theory, content, narrative and discourse, ethnographic, and historical analyses.

Since sociological studies are aimed at understanding and reconstructing the meanings people ascribe to actions and interactions, I feel that the reliability of my study has depended on my abilities to adequately evaluate the range of variation in all my data. Through coding, writing memos, and theoretical sampling, I have been able to test the reasonableness of my analysis of sperm and semen at professional conferences, in the classroom, and in other scholarly peer-reviewed publications so it gains credibility as a reasonable interpretation.

Notes

PREFACE

1. I still have a tattered copy of this book: Andrew Andry and Steven Schepp, *How Babies Are Made* (Boston: Little, Brown, 1968).

2. The organizational mission statement and principles of the Sperm Bank of California are "to ensure that safe and effective reproductive freedom is accessible to everyone":

> Reproductive services will be offered without regard to social, physical and economic circumstances.
>
> Individuals will be empowered to make educated decisions about their options to reproduce.
>
> We are committed to support and advocate for family diversity.
>
> We are committed to providing integrity, quality and excellence in state-of-the-art reproductive health services.

3. Lisa Jean Moore and Matthew Schmidt, "On the Construction of Male Differences: Marketing Variations in Technosemen," *Men and Masculinities* 1:4 (1997): 339–359.

4. These were not paid positions.

5. "ID release" is a term to describe a policy used at certain sperm banks. It means that when a child reaches a certain age, the donor has agreed that identifying variables can be released to the child if he or she wishes to pursue contact with the donor.

6. For recent scientific explorations of ejaculatory disorders, see David J. Ralph and Kevan Wylie, "Ejaculatory Disorders and Sexual Function," *British Journal of Urology* 95:9 (2005): 1181–1186.

7. Kalyani Premkumar, *The Massage Connection: Anatomy and Physiology* (Philadelphia: Lippincott, Williams and Wilkins, 2003), 436.

CHAPTER 1

1. During a campaign by People for the Ethical Treatment of Animals (PETA) to raise awareness about the hazards of drinking cow's milk, the organization attempted to reach out to Spanish-speaking children and their families.

The Eche la Leche (Dump Milk) advertisement depicted a cow with a banner of the slogan. *Echar* is a verb that can mean "discharge," and as Palm Springs Middle School Principal Manny Ferrer stated, "In Spanish, milk can also mean sperm, and well, you can imagine" (Noaki Schwartz, "Anti-Milk Campaign's Spanish Translation Hits Sour Note," *Knight-Ridder Tribune*, March 31, 2003).

2. Jennifer Egan, "Wanted: A Few Good Sperm," *New York Times Magazine*, March 19, 2006, 44.

3. Brooke Shields, *Down Came the Rain: My Journey Through Postpartum Depression* (New York: Hyperion, 2005), 13.

4. David Plotz, *The Genius Factory: The Curious History of the Nobel Prize Sperm Bank* (New York: Random House, 2005).

5. Alex Ginsberg, "$9M 'Seed' Money," *New York Post,* July 25, 2005, front page.

6. Katha Pollitt, "Stiffed," *Nation*, June 13, 2005, 14.

7. "DNA Evidence Frees Man after 20 Years," *CNN,* August 1, 2005, available at http://www.prisonpotpourri.com/COURTSandCASES/DNA/CNN_com%20-%20DNA%20evidence%20frees%20man%20after%2019%20years%20-%20Aug%201,%202005.html (accessed August 1, 2005).

8. Nicholas Bakalar, "Sex, Springs, Prostates and Combat: New Studies, Better Lives," *New York Times,* June 20, 2005, available at www.nytimes.com (accessed June 20, 2005).

9. *Misconceptions,* promotional brochure, available at http://www.wb.com (accessed 2005).

10. Egan, "Wanted: A Few Good Sperm."

11. Emily Martin, "The Egg and the Sperm: How Science Constructed a Romance Based on Stereotypical Male-Female Roles," *Signs* 16(1991): 500. Martin's book *The Woman in the Body* (Boston: Beacon, 1992) further explores human reproduction primarily through the female body.

12. These methods are discussed more thoroughly in the appendix.

13. Masculinity studies are the work of interdisciplinary scholars who aim to disturb the taken-for-granted, essential notions of masculinity as arising from obviously natural male bodies. Masculinity studies have been highly influential to my work, particularly the scholarship of R. W. Connell, *Masculinities* (Berkeley: University of California Press, 1995). See also Michael Kimmel and Michael Messner, *Men's Lives* (Boston: Allyn and Bacon, 1995), and Mike Donaldson, "What Is Hegemonic Masculinity?" *Theory and Society* 22 (1993): 643–657. Hegemonic masculinity helps explain that, while different images of sperm and semen exist in different social worlds, thus producing different versions of masculinity, some of these images of masculinity elevate certain types of men. As a frequently employed term that has traveled widely in its theoretical and descriptive applications, "hegemonic masculinity" has come to mean many dif-

ferent things. Evidence of the production of hegemonic masculinity can be found in narratives from the sports-industrial complex. For example, Mike Messner, M. Dunbar, and D. Hunt, "The Televised Sports Manhood Formula," *Journal of Sports and Social Issues* 24:4 (2000): 380–394, and K. Kusz, "I Want to Be the Minority: The Politics of Youthful White Masculinities in Sport and Popular Culture in 1990s America," *Journal of Sport and Social Issues* 25:4 (2001): 390–416. Because some scholars analyze data as evidence of the existence of an a priori hegemonic masculinity and do not describe its emergent dimensions, hegemonic masculinity can appear both infinite and mysterious. Other scholars attempt to explain the theoretical and political use of the term. This makes the term plastic or slippery as it is tweaked and refined, resulting in several incarnations. What is meant by hegemonic masculinity in this book is a process by which various historically situated sociocultural agents create a commonsense notion of what encompasses the "legitimate masculine." The features of hegemonic masculinity are imposed on all men (and women) by either positive or negative social sanctions. The process of absorbing hegemonic masculinity becomes an always out of reach carrot for men to strive toward in order to reap the patriarchal spoils, although in this competition not all men have the same starting line.

14. For more on this topic, see Londa Schiebinger, *The Mind Has No Sex? Women in the Origins of Modern Science* (Cambridge: Harvard University Press, 1989); Nancy Tuana (ed.), *Feminism and Science* (Bloomington: Indiana University Press, 1989); C. Gallagher and Thomas Laqueur (eds.), *The Making of the Modern Body: Sexuality and Society in the Nineteenth Century* (Berkeley: University of California Press, 1987); Nelly Oudshoorn and Marianne Van Den Wijngaard, "Dualism in Biology: The Case of Sex Hormones," *Women's Studies International Forum* 14:5 (1991): 459–471; and Jennifer Terry, "Lesbians Under the Medical Gaze: Scientists Search for Remarkable Differences," *Journal of Sex Research* 27:3 (1990): 317–339.

15. Kristin Dwight's readings of textual and visual narratives interpret metaphors in which sperm is identified as "an investor and investment . . . diminishing resource and resource-efficient technology." In this important work she suggests that metaphors about sperm have multiple meanings that may mask very real social circumstances and "displace the agency of man onto an alienable bodily substance" ("Sperm Stories: Romantic, Entrepreneurial, and Environmental Narratives About Treating Male Infertility," *Science as Culture* 27 [1997]: 273). See also Barbara Tomlinson, "Phallic Fables and Spermatic Romance: Disciplinary Crossings and Textual Ridicule," *Configurations* 2 (1995): 105–134.

16. Susan Faludi, *Stiffed: The Betrayal of the American Man* (New York: Perennial, 1999), and Christina Hoff Sommers, *The War Against Boys: How Misguided Feminism Is Harming Our Young Men* (New York: Simon and Schuster, 2000).

CHAPTER 2

1. Mary Douglas, *Purity and Danger: An Analysis of the Concepts of Pollution and Taboo* (New York: Routledge, 1966), 163.

2. Ibid.

3. Bk. II, q. 18, art. 1, ad 3, Benziger Brothers edition, published by Fathers of the English Dominican Province, 1947. Thomas Aquinas's *Summa Theologica*, was written and published between 1265 and 1273. The *Summa Contra Gentiles* was written and published between 1258 and 1264.

4. See the historical review of masturbation in Thomas W. Laqueur, *Solitary Sex: A Cultural History of Masturbation* (Cambridge, Mass.: Zone Books, 2003).

5. Clara Pinto-Correia, *The Ovary of Eve: Egg and Sperm and Preformation* (Chicago: University of Chicago Press, 1997), 80.

6. G. J. Barker-Benfield, "The Spermatic Economy: A Nineteenth-Century View of Sexuality," *Feminist Studies* 1:1 (1972): 45–74.

7. *L'Onanisme: Dissertation sur les maladies produites par la masturbation* (Paris: Le Sycomore, 1980); originally published in 1764.

8. John M. Riddle, *Contraception and Abortion from the Ancient World to the Renaissance* (Cambridge: Harvard University Press, 1994).

9. Leeuwenhoek, as quoted in Roger Kempers, "The Tricentennial of the Discovery of Sperm," *Fertility and Sterility* 27:5 (1976): 63.

10. J. L. Prévost and J. B. Dumas, "Deuxième mémoire sur la génération: Rapports de l'oeuf avec la liqueur fécondante," *Annales des Sciences Naturelles* 2 (1824): 129–149.

11. Discussed in John Farley, *Gametes and Spores: Ideas About Sexual Reproduction 1750–1914* (Baltimore: Johns Hopkins University Press,1982).

12. Henry Latou Dickinson, *Human Sex Anatomy* (Baltimore: Williams and Wilkins, 1949), 81.

13. D. Whorton, R. M. Krauss, S. Marshall, and T. H. Milby, "Infertility in Male Pesticide Workers," *Lancet* 2 (1977): 1259–1260; A. J. Wyrobek, L. A. Gordon, J. G. Burkhart, M. W. Francis, R. W. Kapp, G. Letz, L. V. Malling, J. C. Topham, and M. D. Whorton, "An Evaluation of Human Sperm as Indicators of Chemically Induced Alterations of Spermatogenic Function," *Mutation Research* 115 (1983): 173–148; and S. M. Schrader, T. W. Turner, and S. D. Simon, "Longitudinal Study of Semen Quality of Unexposed Workers: Sperm Motility Characteristics" *Journal of Andrology* 12 (1991): 126–131.

14. Richard F. Spark, *The Infertile Male: The Clinician's Guide to Diagnosis and Treatment* (Dordrecht: Kluwer, 1988), 128.

15. As with many aspects of seminal diagnostics, the determination of normal morphology is rife with fractious debate. Because sperm morphology is determined through a visual assessment, it is highly subjective. Further-

more, there are different classification systems of sperm morphology, including the World Health Organization's assessment standards, a method developed by a team of urologists referred to as Kruger or Strict Criteria, and the newer computer-assisted methods. For more on the latter, see J. H. Check, H. G. Adelson, B. R. Schubert, and A. Bollendorf, "Evaluation of Sperm Morphology Using Kruger's Strict Criteria," *Archives of Andrology* 28:1 (1992): 15–17.

16. "Relationship Exists Between Tobacco Chewing and Semen Quality," *Fertility Weekly*, October 10, 2005, 5–6.

17. M. S. Jensen, L. M. Mabeck, G. Toft, A. M. Thulstrup, and J. P. Bonde, "Lower Sperm Counts Following Prenatal Tobacco Exposure," *Human Reproduction* 20:9 (2005): 2559–2566.

18. Y. Gebreeziabher, "Sperm Characteristics of Endurance Trained Cyclists," *International Journal of Sports Medicine* 25:4 (2004): 247–251.

19. E. M. B. Derias, P. Stefanis, A. Drakeley, R. Gazvani, and D. Lewis-Jones, "Growing Concern over the Safety of Using Mobile Phones and Male Fertility," *Archives of Andrology* 52:1 (2006): 9–14.

20. Spark, *Infertile Male*, 130.

21. Kenneth Gannon, Lesley Glover, and Paul Abel, "Masculinity, Infertility, Stigma and Media Reports," *Social Science and Medicine* 59:6 (2004): 1169–1175, and Mary-Claire Mason, *Male Infertility: Men Talking* (New York: Routledge, 1993).

22. D. Macomber and M. Sanders, "The Spermatozoa Count: Its Value in the Diagnosis, Prognosis, and Treatment of Sterility," *New England Journal of Medicine* 200:19 (1929): 981–984.

23. Spark, *Infertile Male*, 60.

24. Marilyn Marx Adelman and Eileen Cahill, *Atlas of Sperm Morphology* (Chicago: ASCP Press Image, 1989).

25. G. L. Moench, discussed in H. L. Dickinson, *Human Sex Anatomy* (Baltimore: Williams and Wilkins, 1949).

26. C. Ezzell, "Picking a Ripe One: A New Strategy for Selecting Sperm," *Journal of NIH Research* 9 (1997): 28–29.

27. Greg Beaubien, "Progress Against Infertility," *American Health*, September 1995, 14.

28. For an analysis of the medicalization of male bodies, the pharmaceutical industry, and male privilege, see Meika Loe, *The Rise of Viagra: How the Little Blue Pill Changed Sex in America* (New York: New York University Press, 2004).

29. To be sure, there are research studies investigating connections between low sperm count, use of ICSI, and increased genetic abnormalities. For an overview of some of the scientific literature on the topic of ICSI and birth defects, see "Promises and Challenges of Intracytoplasmic Sperm Injection," *Fertility Weekly*, February 14, 2005, 5–6.

30. Armand Karow, "Implications of Tissue Banking for Human Reproductive Medicine," in Armand Karow and John Crister (eds.), *Reproductive Tissue Banking: Scientific Principles* (San Diego: Academic Press, 1997): 4–18.

31. Geoff Parker, "Sperm Competition and Its Evolutionary Consequences in the Insects," *Biological Reviews* 45 (1970): 525–567. For an extensive exploration into the history of the theories of sperm competition, see Tim Birkhead, *Promiscuity: An Evolutionary History of Sperm Competition* (Cambridge: Harvard University Press, 2000).

32. Tim Birkhead and A. P. Møller (eds.), *Sperm Competition and Sexual Selection* (San Diego: Academic Press, 1992), and R. L. Smith (ed.), *Sperm Competition and the Evolution of Animal Mating Systems* (New York: Academic Press, 1984).

33. For example, see the literature review in T. K. Shackelford, "Preventing, Correcting, and Anticipating Female Infidelity: Three Adaptive Problems of Sperm Competition," *Evolution and Cognition* 9 (2003): 90–96.

34. Warfare is referred to throughout the text. Baker and Bellis also present their theory as a paradigm shift from Parker's idea of sperm competition as a lottery—see, for example, chapter 2 in Robin Baker and Mark Bellis, *Human Sperm Competition: Copulation, Masturbation and Infidelity* (London: Chapman and Hall, 1995).

35. Robin Baker has experience in this genre as he is also the author of a highly successful trade publication, *Sperm Wars: The Science of Sex* (Collingdale, Pa.: Diane Books, 1996), which relies on some of the same scientific claimmaking.

36. Donna J. Haraway, *Primate Visions: Gender, Race, and Nature in the World of Modern Science* (New York: Routledge, 1989).

37. G. Gottlieb and R. Lickliter, "The Various Roles of Animal Models in Understanding Human Development," *Social Development* 13 (2004): 323.

38. Roger Short, book review of *Human Sperm Competition: Copulation, Masturbation and Infidelity, 1999,* available at http://numbat.murdoch.edu.au/spermatology/rsreview.html (accessed January 12, 2005), and Constance Holden, "No Evidence for the Sperm Wars," *Science* 286:5448 (1999): 2265.

39. Baker and Bellis, *Human Sperm Competition,* xiv.

40. Discussed in Birkhead, *Promiscuity.*

41. Baker and Bellis, *Human Sperm Competition,* 22.

42. Ibid., 1.

43. Ibid., 26.

44. Martin, "Egg and the Sperm."

45. Baker and Bellis, *Human Sperm Competition,* 2.

46. Ibid., 23.

47. Ibid., 251.

48. Ibid., 275, 276.

49. Ibid., 292.

50. For an interactive history of kamikaze fighter pilots, see *Japanese Response*, available at http://motlc.wiesenthal.com/text/x19/xm1943.html (accessed January 15, 2001).

51. Baker and Bellis, *Human Sperm Competition*, 261.

52. Ibid., 23.

53. Ibid., 275.

54. G. G. Gallup, R. L. Burch, M. L. Zappieri, R. A. Parvez, M. L. Stockwell, and J. A. Davis, "The Human Penis as a Semen Displacement Device," *Evolution and Human Behavior* 24 (2003): 277–289. This principle investigator also has conducted research to determine whether semen acts as an antidepressant for women having unprotected sex with men. The data in their study suggest that semen may be protective against depressive symptoms (G. G. Gallup, R. L. Burch, and S. S. M. Platek, "Does Semen Have Antidepressant Properties?" *Archives of Sexual Behavior* 31:3 [2002]: 289–293).

55. Ibid., 278.

56. Aaron T. Goetz, Todd K. Shackelford, Viviana A. Weekes-Shackelford, Harald A. Euler, Sabine Hoier, David P. Schmitt, and Craig W. LaMunyon, "Mate Retention, Semen Displacement, and Human Sperm Competition: A Preliminary Investigation of Tactics to Prevent and Correct Female Infidelity," *Personality and Individual Differences* 38 (2005): 7.

57. T. K. Shackelford, G. J. LeBlanc, V. A. Weekes-Shackelford, A. L. Bleske-Rechek, H. A. Euler, and S. Hoier, "Psychological Adaptation to Human Sperm Competition," *Evolution and Human Behavior* 23 (2002): 123–138.

58. Donald E. Tyler, *The Other Guy's Sperm: The Cause of Cancers and Other Diseases* (Ontario, Ore.: Discovery Books, 1994), 1.

59. Tyler does make an argument that many young girls between three and four who present with urinary tract infections "undoubtedly" (ibid., 84) acquire the illness through contact with the sperm of an abusive male adult. He notes that this is not necessarily through penetrative sex; sitting on the lap of an abuser is a possible mode of exposure.

60. Barker-Benfield, "Spermatic Economy," 53.

61. Michael S. Kimmel, "Men's Responses to Feminism at the Turn of the Century," *Gender and Society* 1:3 (1987): 266.

62. Bob Beale, *Sperm: Amazing Journey of a Tadpole Hero*, 2001, available at http://www.bob.beale.org/chapters.htm (accessed October 14, 2006).

63. Alex Gibrey, *Enron: The Smartest Guys in the Room*, 2005; Richard Dawkins, *The Selfish Gene* (Oxford: Oxford University Press, 1976).

64. Michael Segell was interviewed for his book *Standup Guy: Masculinity That Works* (New York: Villard, 1999) by John Tierney, "Suitable Men: Rare Species Under Study," *New York Times*, June 7, 1999, 84.

65. Tierney, "Suitable Men," 84.

66. Ibid.

67. Lionel Tiger, *The Decline of Males* (New York: St. Martin's, 1999), 2.

68. Quoted in Tierney, "Suitable Men," 85.

69. Tiger, *Decline of Males,* 229.

CHAPTER 3

1. For a comprehensive history of Mary Ware Dennett, see Constance Chen, *Mary Ware Dennett's Pioneering Battle for Birth Control and Sex Education* (New York: New Press, 1996).

2. Copies that are currently available in libraries are dated 1928: Mary Ware Dennett, *The Sex Side of Life: An Explanation for Young People* (Astoria, N.Y.: Published by the author, 1928).

3. Chen, *Dennett's Pioneering Battle,* 171.

4. Dennett, *Sex Side of Life,* 9.

5. John Craig, "'The Sex Side of Life': The Obscenity Case of Mary Ware Dennett," *Frontiers* 15:3 (1995): 145–166.

6. Dorothy Broderick "Sex Education: Books for Young Children," *Top of the News* 34:2 (1978): 159–160.

7. Henry Jenkins (ed.), *The Children's Culture Reader* (New York: New York University Press, 1998), 15.

8. Jacqueline Rose, "The Case of Peter Pan: The Impossibility of Children's Fiction," in Henry Jenkins (ed.), *The Children's Culture Reader* (New York: New York University Press, 1998), 58–66.

9. Bruno Bettleheim, *The Uses of Enchantment: The Meaning and Importance of Fairy Tales* (New York: Knopf, 1976).

10. As reported in Diane Nasatir, "Guide for Reviewing Children's Literature That Includes People with Disabilities: Books Written for Children Three to Five Years of Age," master's thesis, University of Kansas, Lawrence, 2002; Gillian Klein, *Reading into Racism: Bias in Children's Literature and Learning Materials* (London: Routledge, 1985); Council on Interracial Books for Children, *Guidelines for Selecting Bias-Free Textbooks and Storybooks* (New York: Council on Interracial Books for Children, 1980); and E. C. Ayala, "'Poor Little Things' and 'Brave Little Souls': The Portrayal of Individuals with Disabilities in Children's Literature," *Reading Research and Instruction* 39 (1999): 103–107.

11. Richard Kolbe and Joseph La Voie, "Sex-Role Stereotyping in Preschool Children's Picture Books," *Social Psychology Quarterly* 44:4 (1981): 369–374, and Susan Lehr, *Beauty, Brains and Brawn: The Construction of Gender in Children's Literature* (Portsmouth, N.H.: Heinemann, 2001).

12. Bronwyn Davies, *Frogs and Snails and Feminist Tales: Preschool Children and Gender* (Sydney: Allen and Unwin, 1989).

13. Peter Fraser, "How Do Teachers and Students Talk About Television?" in David Buckingham (ed.), *Watching Media Learning: Making Sense of Media Education* (London: Falmer, 1990), 60–78.

14. Davies, *Frogs and Snails and Feminist Tales*, viii.

15. David Buckingham, *Blurring the Boundaries: "Teletubbies" and Children's Media Today*, 2001, available at http://www.br_online.de/jugend/izi/english/e-buck.htm (accessed October 15, 2006).

16. The entire list of sex ed children's books I examined is as follows:

Nicholas Allan, *Where Willy Went* (New York: Knopf, 2004)

Andrew Andry and Steven Schepp, *How Babies Are Made* (Boston: Little, Brown, 1968)

Sue Baker, *The Birds and the Bees* (Swindon, Wiltshire: Child's Play International, 1990)

Joani Blank, *A Kid's First Book About Sex* (San Francisco: Yes Press, 1983)

Laurie Krasny Brown and Marc Brown, *What's the Big Secret? Talking About Sex with Girls and Boys* (Boston: Little, Brown, 1997)

Larry Christenson, *The Wonderful Way Babies Are Made* (Minneapolis: Bethany Backyard, 1982)

Edgar Cockefair and Ada Cockefair, *The Story of You* (Madison, Wisc.: Milam, 1955)

Babette Cole, *Mommy Laid an Egg: or, Where Do Babies Come From?* (San Francisco: Chronicle, 1993)

Joanna Cole, *How You Were Born* (New York: Mulberry, 1984)

Jennifer Davis, *First Comes Love: All About the Birds and the Bees—and Alligators, Possums and People, Too* (New York: Workman, 2001)

Marguerite Kurth Frey, *I Wonder, I Wonder* (St. Louis, Mo.: Concordia, 1967)

Sidonie Matsner Gruenber, *The Wonderful Story of How You Were Born* (Garden City, N.Y.: Hanover House, 1952)

Robie Harris, *It's So Amazing: A Book About Eggs, Sperm, Birth, Babies and Families* (Cambridge, Mass.: Candlewick, 1999)

Ruth Hummel, *Wonderfully Made* (St. Louis, Mo.: Concordia, 1967)

Ruth Hummel, *Where Do Babies Come From? A Series for the Christian Family* (St. Louis, Mo.: Concordia, 1982)

Anne Kubler, *I Know a Secret* (Swindon, Wiltshire: Child's Play International, 1991)

Marion Lerrigo and Helen Southard, *A Story About You* (Chicago: American Medical Association, 1955)

Peter Mayle, *What's Happening to Me? An Illustrated Guide to Puberty* (New York: Kensington, 1975)

Peter Mayle, *Where Did I Come From? The Facts of Life Without Any Nonsense and with Illustrations* (Secaucus, N.J.: Carroll, 1977)

Susan Meredith, *Where Do Babies Come From?* (London: Usborne, 1991)

Lennart Nilsson, *How Was I Born?* (New York: Bantam Doubleday, 1996)

Joan Lowery Nixon, *Before You Were Born* (Huntington, Ind.: Our Sunday Visitor, 1980)

Carolyn Nystrom, *Before I Was Born: Designed for Parents to Read to Their Child at Ages 5 Through 8 (God's Design for Sex)* (Harrisburg, Penn.: Navpress, 1995)

Karl de Schweinitz, *Growing Up: How We Become Alive, Are Born and Grow* (New York: Macmillan, 1965)

Alistar Smith, *How Are Babies Made?* (London: Usborne, 1997)

Norma Stevens, *My Body and Me: For Middle-Age Children* (Nashville: Family Touch, 1993)

Ruth Westheimer, *Who Am I? Where Did I Come From?* (New York: Golden, 2001).

Because most of these books do not have page numbers, I have chosen to cite from the specific books within the body of the chapter's written text.

17. Davis, *First Comes Love*, 14.

18. Although they are outside of the criteria for inclusion in this analysis, it is certainly true that a few sex education books for children and adolescents depict semen outside of the human reproductive motif. For example, Peter Mayle's *Congratulations, You're Not Pregnant: An illustrated Guide to Birth Control* (New York: Macmillan, 1981) includes multiple illustrations of human sperm frustrated in its foiled attempts to woo and romance the egg. A story told through the main illustrated characters of a human penis and vagina, each with arms and legs, uses humor to explain contraception.

19. Harris, *It's So Amazing*, 34.

20. For example, Thomas Laqueur, *Making Sex: Body and Gender from the Greeks to Freud* (Cambridge: Harvard University Press, 1990), and Clara Pinto-Correia, *The Ovary of Eve: Egg and Sperm and Preformation* (Chicago: University of Chicago Press, 1997).

21. Christenson, *The Wonderful Way Babies Are Made*, and Hummel, *Where Do Babies Come From?*, 22.

22. Judith Lorber, *Breaking the Bowls: Degendering and Feminist Change* (New York: Norton, 2005).

CHAPTER 4

Special thanks to Aaron Belkin for this chapter title.

1. Vivien Marx, *The Semen Book* (London: Free Association, 2001).

2. Caroline Aldred, *Divine Sex: The Art of Tantric and Taoist Arts of Conscious Loving* (San Francisco: HarperCollins, 1996).

3. The sanitizing of semen also occurs through industries that make profit by cleaning sperm. Semen banks, as discussed in chapter 5, claim to make semen safe for consumption through processes of technosemen or surveillance and cataloguing. Through some manipulation of seminal ejaculate, semen is safe for consumption in reproductive pursuits without fear of these risks.

4. For recent scientific explorations of ejaculatory disorders, see David J. Ralph and Kevan Wylie, "Ejaculatory Disorders and Sexual Function," *British Journal of Urology* 95:9 (2005): 1181–1186.

5. Premkumar, *Massage Connection*, 436.

6. Interestingly, Tantric and Taoist sex guides, written for the Western audience, explore how semen should be retained as it contains a vital essence called jing. For example, Richard Craze, *The Spiritual Traditions of Sex* (New York: Harmony, 1996), and David and Ellen Ramsdale, *Sexual Energy Ecstasy* (New York: Bantam, 1993). There is a finite amount of jing in a man's body. When men squander their allotment of jing, it depletes them of life energy (chi) and well-being. Manuals provided examples of practices that enable seminal retention while being sexually active, such as particular sexual positions, meditation, and yoga. Peng-Tsu , a Chinese sage and imperial doctor who allegedly lived for 800 years, stated, "Semen must be regarded as a most precious substance. By saving it, a man protects his very life." Quoted in Felice Dunas with Philip Goldberg, *Passion Play* (New York: Riverhead, 1997), 43.

7. Cindy Patton, "Hegemony and Orgasm: Or the Instability of Heterosexual Pornography," *Screen* 30:4 (1989): 1–34.

8. For example, Laura M. Carpenter, *Virginity Lost: An Intimate Portrait of First Sexual Experiences* (New York: New York University Press, 2005).

9. Due to methodological constraints, this chapter primarily relies on heterosexually produced pornography and heterosexually oriented sex workers. That is not to say that viewers or participants in these industries are heterosexual, but it is to bracket the data as produced primarily for a presumed heterosexual audience. Clearly, gay porn or porn featuring men who have sex with men would be a robust site for research about semen and the eroticization of ejaculation.

10. Pamela Paul, *Pornified: How Pornography Is Transforming Our Lives, Our Relationships and Our Families* (New York: Holt, 2005).

11. *Vital Information for Workers and Employers in the Adult Film Industry*, CAL-OSHA, 2003, available at http://www.dir.ca.gov/dosh/adultfilmindustry.html (accessed October 14, 2006).

12. *CAL/OSHA Issues Citations to Adult Film Companies for Failing to Protect Employees from Health Hazards*, September 16, 2004, available at http://www.dir.ca.gov/dirnews/2004/IR2004–10.html (accessed October 14, 2006).

13. Ann Regentin, *What We're Really Watching*, May 26, 2004, available at http://www.cleansheets.com/articles/regentin_05.26.04.shtml (accessed October 14, 2006).

14. Interview with Raylene by Max Gunner, "Seven Inches of Pleasure," *Popsmear Online Magazine*, available at http://www.popsmear.com/lovemaking/seveninches/15.0/index.html (accessed October 14, 2006).

15. Greg Tuck, "Mainstreaming the Money Shot: Representations of Ejaculation in Mainstream American Cinema," in Judith Still (ed.), *Men's Bodies* (Edinburgh: Edinburgh University Press, 2003), 263–279.

16. Linda Williams, *Hard Core: Power, Pleasure and the Frenzy of the Visible* (Berkeley: University of California Press, 1991), 73.

17. Cindy Patton, "Speaking Out: Teaching In," in Diana Fuss (ed.), *Inside/Out: Lesbian Theories, Gay Theories* (New York: Routledge, 1991), 381.

18. Patton, "Hegemony and Orgasm,"105.

19. Cindy Patton, "The Cum Shot: Three Takes on Lesbian and Gay Studies," *Out/Look* 1:3 (1988): 72–76.

20. Ibid., 106.

21. For a history of pornography in the United States, see Joseph Slade, *Pornography in America: A Reference Handbook* (Santa Barbara, Calif.: ABC-CLIO, 2000). As Slade states on page 323: "After the war, the cum shot, the penis ejaculating out of the vagina, became nearly universal."

22. John D'Emilio and Estelle B. Freedman, *Intimate Matters: A History of Sexuality in America* (New York: Harper and Row, 1988), 328.

23. Frederick S. Lane, *Obscene Profits: The Entrepreneurs of Pornography in the Cyber Age* (New York: Routledge, 2000), 34.

24. Paul, *Pornified*.

25. Ibid., 39.

26. Fred Fejes, "Bent Passions: Heterosexual Masculinity, Pornography and Gay Male Identity," *Sexuality and Culture* 6:3 (2002): 95–113.

27. Simon Crompton, "Pornography Increases the Quality of Men's Sperm," *Times* (London), June 18, 2005, 2.

28. For example, Williams, *Hard Core,* and Patton, "Hegemony and Orgasm."

29. These are a collection of descriptions taken from *Reviews*, 2004, available at www.avn.com (accessed October 14, 2006).

30. *Come Again, and Again . . .*, available at http://www.semenex.com/maximwebguide4th.jpg (accessed October 14, 2006).

31. Andrea Dworkin delivered this speech at a conference entitled "Speech, Equality and Harm: Feminist Legal Perspectives on Pornography and Hate Propaganda" at the University of Chicago Law School on March 6, 1993. See also Andrea Dworkin, *Pornography: Men Possessing Women* (New York: Dutton, 1981), and Dworkin, *Intercourse* (New York: Free Press, 1987).

CHAPTER 5

1. Amy Harmon, "First Comes the Baby Carriage," October 13, 2005; Harmon, "Hello, I'm Your Sister: Our Father Is Donor 150," November 20, 2005; Harmon, "Are You My Sperm Donor? Few Clinics Will Say," January 20, 2006, all *New York Times*, available at www.nytimes.com (accessed October 12, 2006).

2. Harmon, "Hello, I'm Your Sister."

3. Council of Europe, *Medically Assisted Procreation and the Protection of the Human Embryo: Comparative Study on the Situation in 39 States* (Strasbourg: Council of Europe, 1998), and W. Weber, "Dutch Sperm Donors Will Remain Anonymous for Another Two Years," *Lancet* 355 (2000): 1249.

4. Harmon, "Hello, I'm Your Sister."

5. For a history of artificial insemination with livestock, see R. H. Foote, "The History of Artificial Insemination: Selected Notes and Notables," *American Society of Animal Science* (2002): 1–10.

6. John Olson, "Present Status of AID and Sperm Banks in the United States," in George David and Wendell Price (eds.), *Human Artificial Insemination and Semen Preservation* (Paris: International Symposium on Artificial Insemination and Semen Preservation, 1979), 424.

7. While there is no obvious documentation that heterosexual couples using a semen bank had to prove they were married through marriage licenses, informational materials from the 1970s and anecdotal evidence use the referents "husbands and wives."

8. J. K. Sherman, "Historical Synopsis of Human Semen Cryobanking," in George David and Wendell Price (eds.), *Human Artificial Insemination and Semen Preservation* (Paris: International Symposium on Artificial Insemination and Semen Preservation, 1979), 100.

9. Frank Buckley, "Insurance Policy: Troops Freezing Sperm," *CNN*, January 30, 2003, available at http://www.cnn.com/2003/HEALTH/01/30/military.fertility/ (accessed October 14, 2006).

10. American Association of Tissue Banks Membership Application.

11. For the full report, see *Guidance for Industry: Eligibility Determination for Donors of Human Cells, Tissues, and Cellular and Tissue-Based Products*, May 2004, available at http://www.fda.gov/cber/gdlns/tissdonor.pdf (accessed October 14, 2006).

12. Boston Women's Health Book Collective, *The New Our Bodies, Ourselves* (New York: Touchstone, 1992), 387.

13. Scandinavian Cyrobank, available at http://www.scandinavian cryobank.com (accessed October 14, 2006).

14. Pre-sex selection involves centrifuging semen in order to separate and sort sperm cells to increase the likelihood of conceiving a male or a female.

15. All prices are based on 2006 data.

16. *FDA Set to Ban Gay Men as Sperm Donors,* May 5, 2005, available at http://www.msnbc.msn.com/id/7749977 (accessed October 14, 2006).

17. Ibid.

18. Steve Epstein, *Impure Science: AIDS, Activism and the Politics of Knowledge* (Berkeley: University of California Press, 1996).

19. These websites are http://www.cryobank.com, http://www.fertilityctr.com, and http://www.thespermbankofca.org (accessed October 14, 2006).

20. This website is http://www.cryos.dk/history.asp (accessed January 12, 2005).

21. Information summarized from an editorial titled, "Eggs Shared, Given, and Sold," *Lancet* 362:9382 (2003): 413, and New York State Department of Health and Bernadine Healy, "The High Cost of Eggs," *U.S. News and World Report,* January 13, 2003, 44.

22. Harmon, "Hello, I'm Your Sister," and Harry Fisch, *The Male Biological Clock* (New York: Free Press, 2005).

23. Harmon, "First Comes the Baby Carriage."

24. For example, Maggie Gallagher, *The Age of Unwed Mothers: Is Teen Pregnancy the Problem?* (New York: Institute for American Values, 1999).

25. *Single Mothers by Choice,* available at http://mattes.home.pipeline.com/ (accessed October 14, 2006).

26. "Unmarried U.S. Women Delivered Record 1.47M Infants in 2004, Report Says," National Center for Health Statistics Report, November 2, 2005, available at http://www.medicalnewstoday.com (accessed October 14, 2006).

27. "Feds: 1.5 Million Babies Born to Unwed Moms in '04," *USA Today,* October 31, 2005, available at http://www.usatoday.com/news/nation/2005-10-31-unwed-families_x.htm (accessed October 14, 2006).

28. For an exploration into the history of American sperm banking, with particular attention to eugenic implications, see Cynthia Daniels and Janet Golden, "Procreative Compounds: Popular Eugenics, Artificial Insemination and the Rise of the American Sperm Banking Industry," *Journal of Social History* 38:1 (2004): 5–27.

29. Quote from transcript of anonymous interview with West Coast sperm bank administrator, September 14, 1998.

30. The goals of the Human Genome Project purport to map the human body's makeup and have the potential to cause a resurgence of eugenic practices, such as constructing designer babies of the preferred gender, coloring, and size.

31. From http://www.mannotincluded.com (accessed March 1, 2004), now called http://www.fertility4life.com (accessed October 14, 2006).

32. As Matt Schmidt and I have previously argued, sperm banks are active participants in erasing the biological and social differences between sperm cells

and the men who donated them. Instead of identifying with the sperm, clients are encouraged to identify with the specific men through their physical characteristics, personalities, and desires. As we stated earlier, "For example a donor who likes to play the trombone, ballroom dance and read Chaucer may culturally indicate healthier semen than a donor who enjoys slam dancing, riding Harley motorcycles, and body piercing. The Lamarckian assumption of the inheritance of acquired characteristics is both recreated and sustained in these catalogues. Through a dialectical process, semen banks invest semen with social characteristics" (Lisa Jean Moore and Matthew Schmidt, "On the Construction of Male Differences: Marketing Variations in Technosemen," *Men and Masculinities* 1:4 [1999]: 345).

33. Josephine Quintavalle, *Internet Sperm Bank for Lesbians,* Comment on Reproductive Ethics, June 24, 2002, available at http://news.bbc.co.uk/2/hi/health/2062212.stm (accessed October 14, 2006).

34. *Father Facts,* available at http://www.fatherhood.org/ (accessed October 14, 2006).

35. For example, D. Rosenthal, G. K. Leigh, and R. Elardo, "Home Environment of Three to Six Year Old Children from Father-Absent and Two-Parent Families," *Journal of Divorce* 9:2 (1985): 41–48, and D. Wenk, C. L. Hardesty, C. S. Morgan, and S. L. Blair, "The Influence of Parental Involvement on the Well-being of Sons and Daughters," *Journal of Marriage and the Family* 56:1 (1994): 229–234.

36. *NFI Mission and Accomplishments,* 1994–2006, available at http://www.fatherhood.org (accessed October 14, 2006).

37. Wade Horn, "Save the Dads," *Jewish World Review,* January 5, 2000.

38. *President Bush Speaks at Fourth National Summit on Fatherhood,* June 7, 2001, available at http://www.whitehouse.gov/news/releases/2001/06/20010607–3.html (accessed October 14, 2006).

39. *Mrs. Bush's Remarks at the National Fatherhood Initiative Awards,* April 19, 2005, available at http://www.whitehouse.gov/news/releases/2005/04/20050419–11.html (accessed October 14, 2006).

40. J. Leo, "Promoting No-Dad Families: Artificial Insemination and Single Women," *U.S. News and World Report,* May 15, 1995, 26.

41. Michael Kimmel, *Manhood in America: A Cultural History* (New York: Free Press, 1996), and John Stoltenberg, *Refusing to Be a Man: Essays on Sex and Justice* (New York: Penguin, 1990). In the past decade, there have been several critical analyses of the fatherhood rights movement. For an overview, see Michael Kimmel, "Fatherhood Responsibility Movement," in Michael Kimmel and Amy Aronson (eds.), *Men and Masculinities: A Social, Cultural and Historical Encyclopedia* (Santa Barbara, Calif.: ABC-CLIO, 2004): 279–281, and Anna Gavanas, "Father's Rights," in ibid., 289–290. For a critique of some of the essential attitudes of fathers, see Louise Silverstein and Carl F. Auerbach, "Deconstructing the Essential Father," *American Psychologist* 54:6 (1999): 397–405. For

an overview of the scholarship on fatherhood, see William Marsiglio, Paul Amato, Randal D. Day, and Michael Lamb, "Scholarship on Fatherhood in the 1990s and Beyond," *Journal of Marriage and the Family* 62 (2000): 1173–1191. For the politics of fatherhood, see Cynthia R. Daniels (ed.), *Lost Fathers: The Politics of Fatherlessness in America* (New York: St. Martin's, 1998).

42. Michael S. Kimmel, "The New Men's Movement: Retreat and Regression with America's Weekend Warriors," *Feminist Issues* 13:2 (1993): 19.

43. Trish Wilson, *Deconstructing Fatherhood Propaganda*, 1999, available at http://www.xyonline.net/deconfatherhood.shtml (accessed October 14, 2006).

44. David Blankenhorn, *Fatherless America: Confronting Our Most Urgent Social Problem* (New York: Harper, 1996), 176.

45. Ibid.

46. Ibid.

47. For statistics and data on child support collections and enforcement, see *OCSE Annual Report to Congress, FY 2002/FY 2003,* available at http://www.acf.hhs.gov/programs/cse/prgrpt.htm (accessed October 14, 2006).

48. Sherry Ortner, "Is Female to Male as Nature Is to Culture?" in Michelle Rosaldo and Louise Lamphere (eds.), *Woman, Culture and Society* (Stanford, Calif.: Stanford University Press, 1974), 67–89.

CHAPTER 6

1. Transcripts from Department of Justice news conference on March 11, 2003, with John Ashcroft, attorney general, including testimony from Kellie Greene, founder and director of Speaking out About Rape, Inc.

2. Margrit Shildrick, *Leaky Bodies and Boundaries: Feminism, Postmodernism and (Bio)ethics* (New York: Routledge, 1997).

3. Up-to-the-minute statistics on the number of profiles in the database are provided in the Combined DNA Indexing System (CODIS). Federal Bureau of Investigation, August 2006, available at http://www.fbi.gov/hq/lab/codis/clickmap.htm (accessed October 14, 2006).

4. Ibid.

5. Michel Foucault, *The Birth of the Clinic* (New York: Pantheon, 1973), and Foucault, *Discipline and Punish* (New York: Pantheon, 1977).

6. Barry Steinhardt, testimony before a House Judiciary Sub-Committee on Crime, March 2000, available at http://www.aclu.org/privacy/medical/14850leg20000323.html (accessed October 14, 2006).

7. Pilar Ossorio and Troy Duster, "Race and Genetics: Controversies in Biomedical, Behavioral and Forensic Sciences," *American Psychologist* 60:1 (2005): 115–128.

8. James A. Gilmer and David J. van Alstyne, *The First 100 Hits: Forensic-Offender Matches on the New York State DNA Data Bank,* National Criminal Justice Reference Service and New York State Division of Criminal Justice Services,

January 2002, available at http://criminaljustice.state.ny.us/crimnet/ojsa/ 100_hits/2002 (accessed September 14, 2005).

9. For example, Congressman Jerrold Nadler's Rape Kit DNA Analysis Backlog Elimination Act (S. 231), 2002, and Rape Kits and DNA Evidence Backlog Elimination Act (S. 149), 2003, provide additional funds to process backlogged rape kits until 2009.

10. Joanne Richard, "If All Else Fails, Spy on Your Kids," *Lloydminster Meridian Booster*, April 10, 2005, A18.

11. "The Innocence Project at the Benjamin N. Cardozo School of Law at Yeshiva University, founded by Barry C. Scheck and Peter J. Neufeld in 1992, is a non-profit legal clinic and criminal justice resource center. We work to exonerate the wrongfully convicted through postconviction DNA testing; and develop and implement reforms to prevent wrongful convictions. This Project only handles cases where postconviction DNA testing can yield conclusive proof of innocence" (The Innocence Project, 2006, available at www.innocence project.org [accessed October 14, 2006]).

12. Certainly, the role of paternity testing is another use of DNA forensics that is highly linked to tropes of masculinity. However, since DNA testing for paternity cases is after sperm and semen have been implicated (the seed has been spilled), it is not useful to our analysis to look at these tests, which rely on blood-testing technologies. For an analysis of the actor network created through paternity testing, see Arthur Daemmrich, "The Evidence Does Not Speak for Itself: Expert Witnesses and the Organization of DNA-Typing Companies," *Social Studies of Science* 28:5–6 (1998): 741–772.

13. For example, David G. Horn, *The Criminal Body: Lombroso and the Anatomy of Deviance* (New York: Routledge, 2003).

14. Troy Duster, *Backdoor to Eugenics* (New York: Routledge, 1990).

15. Hilton J. Kobus, E. Silenieks, and J. Scharnberg, "Improving the Effectiveness of Fluorescence for the Detection of Semen Stains," *Journal of Forensic Science* 47:4 (2002): 819–823.

16. Lisa Forman Cody, "The Politics of Reproduction: From Midwives' Alternative Public Sphere to the Public Spectacle of Man-Midwifery," *Eighteenth-Century Studies* 32:4 (1999): 477–495.

17. G. J. Barker-Benfield, *The Horrors of the Half-Known Life: Male Attitudes Toward Women and Sexuality in Nineteenth-Century America* (New York: Routledge, 2000).

18. Mathiew Orfila from 1827, quoted in R. E. Gaensslen, *Sourcebook in Forensic Serology, Immunology, and Biochemistry* (Washington, D.C.: National Institute of Justice, 1983), 74.

19. A. Florence, translation of "Du sperme et des taches de sperme en medecine legale," in *Archives d'Anthropologie Criminelle de Criminologie et de Psychologie Normale et Pathologique* 10 (1896): 417–434, quoted in R. E. Gaensslen,

Sourcebook in Forensic Serology, Immunology, and Biochemistry (Washington, D.C.: National Institute of Justice, 1983), 112.

20. Ellen Bayuk Rosenman, "Body Doubles: The Spermatorrhea Panic," *Journal of the History of Sexuality* 12:3 (2003): 373.

21. Quoted in Gaensslen, *Sourcebook*, 104.

22. Ibid., 105.

23. Andre A. Moenssens, *Fingerprinting Techniques* (Florence, Ky.: Chilton, 1971).

24. Paul L. Kirk, *Crime Investigation* (New York: Interscience, 1953), 4.

25. Quoted in Gaensslen, *Sourcebook*, 104.

26. Kirk, *Crime Investigation*, 95.

27. Ibid., 210.

28. Ibid., 668.

29. *Crime Case Closed Forensic Science*, available at www.bbc.co.uk/pront/crime/caseclosed/colinpitchfork.shtml (accessed October 14, 2006).

30. Due to the unique biological properties of sperm cells, DNA testing of semen samples uses slightly different protocols from testing other biological materials, such as saliva or blood. In 1980, David Botstein and coworkers were the first to exploit these variations found between people; the type of variation they used is called restriction fragment length polymorphism, or RFLP (Norah Rudin and Keith Inman, *An Introduction to Forensic DNA Analysis*, 2nd ed. [Boca Raton, Fla.: CRC Press, 2001], 21). RFLP identifies a specific restriction enzyme that reveals a pattern difference between the DNA fragment sizes in individual organisms. For more information, see *ISCID Encyclopedia*, International Society for Complexity, Information, and Design, 2001–2005, http://www.iscid.org/encyclopedia (accessed October 14, 2006). In 1983 Alec Jeffreys, a professor at the University of Leicester, found that these repeat sequences, contain "core" sequences, which opened the way for the development of probes that contain the core sequences.

31. Currently two procedures are used in forensics to conduct DNA testing: RFLP and PCR, or polymerase chain reaction. PCR is a process mediated by an enzyme that synthesizes new DNA from an existing template to yield millions of copies of a desired DNA sequence (Rudin and Inman, *Forensic DNA*, 211). PCR is the standard in the field, preferred because smaller and more degraded samples can be tested and it is more cost effective.

32. Personal communication with Michael Lynch, January 2005.

33. Sharon Krum, "Private Investigations," *Guardian*, November 15, 2001, available at http://www.guardian.co.uk (accessed September 26, 2003); Carlene Hempel, "TV's Whodunit Effect . . ." *Boston Globe Magazine*, September 2, 2003, 13.

34. O. Dyer, "DNA Evidence May Have Been Misleading to Courts," *British Medical Journal* 308 (1994): 874–875.

35. Thomas L. Dumm, "Leaky Sovereignty: Clinton's Impeachment and the Crisis of Infantile Republicanism," *Theory and Event* 2:4 (1999): 16.

36. "The Science of the Brief Encounter," *Sports Illustrated,* September 6, 2004, available at http://sportsillustrated.cnn.com/2004/magazine/08/31/scorecard0906/ (accessed October 14, 2006).

37. Kirk Johnson, "Bryant Case Alters Rape Counselor's Work," *New York Times,* August 22, 2004, available at www.nytimes.com (accessed September 6, 2004).

38. As of mid-2006, *CSI* was broadcast in 175 countries, making it the most-watched television program in the world, according to Peter Sussman, chief executive of Alliance Atlantis, a Canadian production studio that co-owns the series with CBS. For more on the show, see Bill Carter, "From Creator of 'C.S.I.,' Testimonials to Himself," *New York Times,* August 11, 2003, available at http://www.nytimes.com/2003/08/11/business/media/11TUBE.html (accessed September 6, 2004).

39. From "One Hit Wonder" (Season 3, Episode 14):

Nick: Hey, Grissom. Got what looks like a semen stain. It's crusted, it's not fresh.

From "Primum Non Nocere" (Season 2, Episode 16):

Grissom (investigating the bedroom of a victim): "Well, Jane may play hockey, but her sheets are distinctly female."
Sara (using a UV light): "There are semen stains everywhere. Not very Victoria Secret."

40. *So, Why Do You Have This Big Semen Stain in Your Underwear?* Evergreen Industries, 1999–2006, available at www.getcheckmate.com (accessed January 12, 2005).

41. *True Semen Detective Stories,* Evergreen Industries, available at http://www.getcheckmate.info/testimonials.htm (accessed January 12, 2005).

42. Sharon Krum, "Private Investigations," *Guardian,* November 15, 2001, available at http://www.guardian.co.uk (accessed September 26, 2003).

43. "Testimonials," *Infidelity Today,* 1999–2004, available at www.infidelitytestingtoday.com (accessed January 12, 2005).

44. Ibid.

45. "Testing a Woman," *Checkmate,* available at http://infidelitycheck.us/testing_a-_woman.html (accessed January 12, 2005).

46. Ibid.

47. "Testimonials."

48. "Testing a Woman."

49. Ibid.

50. "At Home Hints," *ClueFinders,* available at www.cluefinders.tripod.com (accessed January 12, 2005).

51. Dorothy Nelkin and Lori Andrews, "DNA Identification and Surveillance Creep," *Sociology of Health and Illness* 21:5 (1999): 700.

52. *New York State DNA Databank Qualifying Offenses*, Department of Criminal Justice, available at www.criminaljustice.state.ny.us/forensic/ (accessed October 14, 2006).

53. *Statement from Governor Pataki*, New York State Office of Governor, March 2, 2004, available at www.state.ny.us/governor/press/year04/march2-2-04.htm (accessed October 14, 2006).

CHAPTER 7

1. Adele E. Clarke, "Social Worlds/Arenas Theory as Organizational Theory," in David Maines (ed.), *Social Organization and Social Process: Essays in Honor of Anselm Strauss* (New York: Aldine de Gruyter, 1991), 119–158.

2. This scenario is briefly alluded to in the film *Gattaca*. This science fiction film explores a world of genetic perfection; the main character is disabled in part because he was a love child, conceived without the benefit of genetic engineering.

METHODS APPENDIX

1. Lisa Jean Moore, "'It's Like You Use Pots and Pans to Cook. It's the Tool': The Technologies of Safer Sex," *Science, Technology and Human Values* 22:4 (1997): 434–471; Lisa Jean Moore, "'I Was Just Learning the Ropes': Becoming a Practitioner of Safer Sex," *Applied Behavioral Science Review* 5:1 (1997): 41–58; and Lisa Jean Moore, "'All in My Bag of Tricks': Turning a Trick with the Appropriate(d) Technology," in Ron Eglash, Jennifer Crossiant, Giovanna Di Chiro, and Rayvon Fouché (eds.), *Appropriating Technology: Vernacular Science and Social Power* (Minneapolis: University of Minnesota Press, 2003), 51–62.

2. For example, Judith Levine, *Harmful to Minors: The Perils of Protecting Children from Sex* (Minneapolis: University of Minnesota Press, 2002).

3. Anselm Strauss and Juliet Corbin, *Basics of Qualitative Research* (Newbury Park, Calif.: Sage, 1990); Anselm Strauss and Juliet Corbin, "Grounded Theory Methodology: An Overview," in Norm Denzin and Yvonne Lincoln (eds.), *Handbook in Qualitative Research* (London: Sage, 1994), 1–18; and Barney Glaser and Anselm Strauss, *The Discovery of Grounded Theory* (Chicago: Aldine, 1967).

4. Strauss and Corbin, "Grounded Theory Methodology," 273.

5. R. P. Weber, *Basic Content Analysis* (Newbury Park, Calif.: Sage, 1990); Karl Krippendorff, *Content Analysis: An Introduction to Its Methodology* (Beverly Hills, Calif.: Sage, 1980); and R. Rosengren, *Advances in Content Analysis* (Beverly Hills, Calif.: Sage, 1981).

6. Strauss and Corbin, *Basics of Qualitative Research*, 61.

7. Barney Glaser, *Theoretical Sensitivity: Advances in the Methodology of Grounded Theory* (Mill Valley, Calif.: Sociology Press, 1978), 39.

8. Norman Denzin, *The Research Act: A Theoretical Introduction to Sociological Methods* (Englewood, N.J.: Prentice Hall, 1989), 270.

9. Ibid., 12.

10. Ibid., 241.

Index

About the Author

Lisa Jean Moore is Associate Professor of Sociology and Women's Studies and Coordinator of the Gender Studies Program at Purchase College, SUNY. Her most recent book, *Gendered Bodies: Feminist Perspectives*, is coauthored with Judith Lorber. She is presently writing *Missing Bodies* with Monica Casper.